D0064914

MY MINIATURE WORLD

By Eric T. Rawlins

Published by

MELROSE BOOKS

An Imprint of Melrose Press Limited
St Thomas Place, Ely
Cambridgeshire
CB7 4GG, UK
www.melrosebooks.com

FIRST EDITION

Cover designed by Serena Rawlins

ISBN 978-1-906050-84-9

Printed and bound in Great Britain by:
CPI Antony Rowe, Chippenham, Wiltshire

FOREWORD

This book is dedicated to the spirit of the Reverend Edward Beal, whose railway modelling books, published before and after World War II, remain the essential guides and inspiration for all practical modellers of the steam age in Britain.

CONTENTS

CONTENTS (CONT.)

INTRODUCTION

T he story told in these pages describes just how valuable to my general journey through life has been my fascination with transport: trains, aircraft, boats, and even road vehicles. The reader may see how my childhood interests developed into concern, by the late 1940s, to capture for posterity the railways system from late Victorian times to Nationalisation – by reproduction in model form. The concept became the 'Railways in Miniature Museum' (RiMM), and the story of its growth, well before the days of full size 'preservation' schemes, follows.

Over the years, the development of the collection has followed a number of interesting phases, for which only now is it possible to look back and enumerate, and which the existing models are a reality to stop the clock for new generations. The initial concept of period, 1880 to 1947, has been followed to about 98 per cent of intention. The original idea of twenty representative trains stemmed from the likely maximum size of a permanent display area, and also for the need to have 'spare' locomotives and stock to replace those 'in shops' for maintenance, rebuilding etc. Early in the 1940s, research indicated the incredible mass of material covered by the sixty-seven years 'middle ages' time span for RiMM. This postulated that the trains to be reproduced must (a) have significant historical importance socially, as well as in a technical sense and (b) as far as practicable, duplication of either full size or other model collections in the public domain be avoided.

In practice, this has meant almost shunning the Midland Railway, so well represented by Leicester City Museum and (less easy to avoid duplication!) the more Catholic, but shorter timescale, which Roye England's 'Pendon' would, with many expert constructors, eventually achieve. He and I exchanged correspondence so it was not a case of either of us 'going it alone'. David Jenkinson's collection of models, under the York Railway Museum development, represented a new concept well after RiMM had begun – but, he had the advantage of a **budget**! In the main, therefore, my scheme sought to avoid reproducing in miniature what was **known** to exist full size, even in the then completely scattered 'British Railways' hands or in museums. Since RiMM predates all the preserved railways in concept, it is inevitable that enthusiasts have been able to rescue from scrap yards full size examples of what had been thought to have been destroyed!

LOCOMOTIVES

Throughout the existence of the railways the primary key to success or failure has always been dependable motive power. Without distorting the relative importance of these matters it was, nevertheless, a fact of significance that much time and engineering energy had been applied to improving steam engine efficiency between 1880 and 1947. Not all developments were successful, but failure was usually partial and seldom solely technical in nature. As ever, seeking to avoid what the whim of fate had preserved full size, RiMM went down the following path in locomotive reincarnation. Examples will be seen of (i) 'compounding' – using the steam to work in both high and low pressure cylinders, (ii) extended use of 'superheaters' to dry the steam, (iii) the eight-coupled engine for haulage of 1,000-ton freight trains, (iv) the ultimate development of the 'four-coupled' engine, (v) turn of the century use of the 'Atlantic' 4-4-2 wheel arrangement, (vi) development of the 4-6-0 and the 'Pacific' 4-6-2 express passenger locomotives and (vii) the extensive 'rebuilds' to meet the urgent needs of World Wars I and II, at home and abroad.

COACHING STOCK

The passenger locomotive choice reproduced, either 'as built' or modified as at a particular date, influenced the choice of the contemporary passenger carrying vehicles to be shown. Representatives of four-, six- and eight-wheeled stock abound and a train for each of the 'Big Four' post-1923 companies is included together with a selection of the Pullman Car Company vehicles as contracted to the Southern and London North Eastern Railways. Development can be traced of stock initially comprising single, isolated compartments, later linked to lavatory accommodation, the corridors eventually extending the length of the coach and then by through gangways, providing access to the adjoining vehicle and the entire train. Lighting was successively by oil, gas-oil, gas, and direct current electricity, generated by axle driven dynamos and stored in batteries slung under the vehicles.

Accommodation for first, second and third class passengers was at one time offered, together with sleeping, dining and buffet cars. The national full size collection is especially strong in Royal and semi-Royal coaches, which led a cloistered life with the companies. However, RiMM was led by fate, as later recounted, to recreate the South Eastern & Chatham Railway (SE & CR) Royal Train of 1914, and this presents a spectacular glimpse of the pinnacle of decorated grandeur at the close of an age which had vanished for ever in the turmoil of World War I.

PASSENGER STOCK

Railwaymen made a distinction between horse boxes, carriage and scenery trucks, special cattle vans, milk, fish, fruit, newspaper vehicles etc, which were 'fitted' with through-compressed air or vacuum brakes, and steam heating pipes; and the coaching stock (which carried passengers) and the freight wagons. All such vehicles ran in passenger carrying trains, or separately, as convenient for the formation, for example, of Christmas parcel traffic or moving the Bertram Mills Circus. Some such four-wheeled vehicles were subjected to restrictions concerned with their wheelbase, the stiffness of springing, depth of wheel flange etc. Basically, little known or ignored by the average person, this category of stock earned valuable revenue, charged at 'passenger' rates. The visitor to RiMM will see many of these vehicles in wide variety, both in the liveries of the pre-Grouping and post-Grouping companies. Look out for the 'tail traffic' which may be attached at either end of passenger carrying trains.

SPECIAL FREIGHT STOCK

Goods stock built for special purposes, rather than for the carriage of general merchandise, minerals etc has long been a feature of the railways and, indeed, as 'common carriers', they were expected to provide such facilities. In emergencies, as in the World Wars, the government of the day sponsored special War Department trucks for the carriage of armoured fighting vehicles. Even in 1996 the Army has rediscovered that all but their heaviest tanks can most economically be moved by the railways! RiMM has paid particular attention to this class of stock and a most extraordinary collection of unusual vehicles, with equally fascinating contemporary loads, offer a unique historical study for both the casual visitor and the keen student of times past.

FREIGHT STOCK

What the general public refers to as 'goods trucks' falls under the United States influence on British railways research and development at the turn of the century; so a railwayman in Britain uses the 'freight stock' expression. Although it was the vast coal and other mineral traffic which provided the basic revenue for most railways, and the RiMM collection shows some representative examples owned by both collieries and retailers, repetition of the long trains of virtually identical wagons was considered unnecessary within the practicable limitations of the museum concept.

RAILWAYS AT WAR

It was inescapable that RiMM had to include a tribute to the railways of Britain and the men and women who, by sheer guts and effort, literally won both World Wars, 1914–18 and 1939–45. Remember that road transport in 1914 was still developing technically; and in the 1939 struggle, Britain depended **desperately** upon the Merchant Navy for importing oil, petrol, rubber and many finished products from the United States. Movement of personnel, animals and stores by the home produced power of coal, fed either into locomotives or electricity power station boilers, was the salvation of the country. Fascinating evidence of stores, vehicles etc so conveyed keeps coming to light, and representative freight trains of both World Wars continue to grow in length on RiMM. This difficulty of obtaining information was, of course, against a background of extraordinary **security**, during which only official photography was allowed. Anyone able to obtain film otherwise and attempting to expose it in railway localities would most likely be shot! Ambulance trains were supplied by the companies in both conflicts. Indeed, as with humans, some vehicles served in both wars. RiMM has chosen to portray an LNER example from World War II, because only in that war were the British pushed out of mainland Europe, via Dunkirk; and it fell to the railways to move a third of a million service personnel away from the Luftwaffe and the South Coast, in an endless succession of special trains and in numbers quite impossible to handle by road.

CHAPTER ONE

The Nineteen-Thirties

It is hardly possible to recall, as I write in 1996, just how soon mechanical models of all types became a fascination for me. Before going to school, at five years of age, I played with neighbouring children and the usual items of metal animals, of zoo and farm, were laid out among the 'Lotts' bricks and wooden equivalent. In about 1930, I had a circle of track with a 00 gauge (five-eighths of an inch) imported from Germany where it was made to the designs of Henry Greenly and W. J. Bassett-Lowke. I recall this as comprising one four-coupled engine and two four-wheeled coaches. Next door, after the Aitkinses departed for Walsall, the taxi-driving Mr May and family arrived. He built a large garage and because of foolish planning restrictions, had to place it where it took much of the light from the garden of our house at 221 Thornton Road. In this garage lived a 1937 Jaguar SS 100 roadster, worth today in good condition probably £70,000! Hugh May was the son – a little blond haired lad, not allowed to play with the rougher neighbours, but to whom I was permitted access. Indeed, his young mother, expecting another baby, rather welcomed my five-year-old presence as companion to Hugh, who had a magnificent United States-made Lionel freight train. This was AC electric powered, had a whistle and was quite beyond my pocket. But I had some Hornby O gauge pieces by about 1938: two locomotives both so high geared in clockwork as to be a permanent disappointment on the 2ft radius curves.

At 68 Park Lane, Croydon, Gerald Blake and I spent many summer Sundays in the relatively huge L shaped garden around the rear of the Meeting House. Here, his Hornby track, often covered with earth over the sleepers, ran in long twisting lengths – usually as a military railway – in conjunction with his large collection of Brittains' soldiers. Of course, the real railways were critical in supplying the armies during World War I and the bound volumes of that conflict's proceedings, well illustrated, were housed in a small rotating bookcase at No. 68. When

1

Gerald was away from home, I would study these books as my parents played cards with Jack and Hannah Blake. Just one of the presents I received one Christmas was a wooden signal box from Jack's personal assistant 'Brownie' at work. This had the window frames punched out from a card-mache strip. It had a hinged roof for the levers I would never be able to afford, for any permanent place for the models to 7mm scale was quite out of the question. The floor of our front room was my world but it had to be cleared away each time the trains ran.

One day, Dad, returning from his insurance round, came scooting his bike up the path and had an announcement to make. In the 'middle-class' area of his clients, in the Fairlands Road location, a contributor had just built an extensive Hornby layout for his son. This must have been just before the war. We were invited to visit and ducked beneath the large oval of tracks laid in Hornby's special steel track of large radius. Upon this breathtaking display was 'Princess Elizabeth' – the pride of the company's products – costing I think five guineas (£5 5s) – almost a fortnight's wages for a man at the time. To see a Hornby model with the correct wheelbase as a 'Pacific' 4-6-2 plus a train of LMS corridor coaches was a real thrill to me. I think the 'Schools' locomotive 'Eton' was also operating: all electric, even if three-rail, but, such power – comparable to the Lionel set, I felt.

On visits to Mr Cook, ex-Royal Flying Corps pilot and now our dentist in the London Road, Norbury, I would occasionally treat myself to a Hornby ls 6d van from the rather superior model shop nearby. But, the disappointing performance of the too high geared clockwork engines only exasperated me and my interest, by 1939, had turned to the new electric Hornby Dublo 0-6-2 tank engine sets and the Trix Twin 0-4-0 Ts being imported from Germany by Bassett-Lowke. The '0' gauge stuff was sold and Mum and I set off to Croydon to see what was on offer – toys already becoming in short supply. At Halfords, just our side of West Croydon Station, we looked at the Dublo but were, I think, put off by the extras – transformer/rectifier – required. However, at either Alders or Grant's the die was cast and we purchased a Trix set in an over-large box with 'space for your next train' and staggered home. I believe we walked both ways – a perfectly natural thing to do in pre-war days.

Both AC Trix and DC Hornby were 3-rail systems and there

2

is no doubt that the latter had the more authentic track base, over the highly efficient Bakelite moulding of Trix. Not having the cash to buy another train, I used the 'spare' third rail to feed a pick-up and work a home-made magnet which would uncouple the trains – despite being AC fed! This, and a 2-colour signal was also home-made and I managed a simple track circuit so that if the light was 'red' no power reached the engine. By now the early wartime shortages of 1939–40 were beginning to bite. Dad managed to get a sheet of plywood about 2ft 6in by 4ft, which was from dismantled stage scenery! This, with a three-quarter inch square frame at the edges, gave me my first baseboard, on top of my bedroom chest of drawers. A cycling holiday to Horley (Smallfields actually) gave us a break in 1940 and I made two trips to Guildford to buy a few more track sections. I recall having to buy 'curves only' on the first occasion and arguing with the shopkeeper for some 'straights' the next time!

At Christmas, I bought the last Hornby Dublo van item in Kennards' very shrunken toy department. It was non-insulated and not suitable for the Trix set, but perhaps illustrates just how shortages affected our behaviour! None of my immediate neighbours were modellers and Rex Nicholls, being at 6 Harcourt Road, and myself gravitated together when school was done. His father made a large model yacht, some three feet in length, with its own stand to keep the keel clear of the ground. We took it over to the Mitcham Common large pond one gusty day and, most unfortunately, the wind caught it on the stand and it crashed over – splitting the side. It was a most irate father who greeted our return and I don't know whether he effected the fairly modest repair involved. Although wartime shortages made toys even rarer than usual in homes where there was little cash to spare (very few wives with children had jobs even for war work) the coal or coke range had to be kept burning. This meant that every home had a 'wood box' into which all pieces from bombsites etc would await final chopping to size. Rex and I became expert at raiding this source – mainly for deal – from which he would make excellent tanks and civil aircraft – the latter for his imagined post-war airline. He had the patience to make three of each type and at sixteen years of age he was working for 'Redwings' at Croydon Airport. Amazing to both of us, they were sub-contracting units for the obsolete Fairey Battle! I was much taken by the design of tea clippers, which appeared on cigarette cards – always a good source of information for us lads. I discovered that by shaping a hull of about four inches in length, out of solid white wood, and sticking a safety razor blade part-way in as a keel, a respectable floating model resulted. The three masts each had a set of sails cut from old handkerchief material in one piece, snipping out the space between the cross-trees, to which they were glued. These boats we took to sail on the water-filled trenches dug across the common to trip up the Junkers 52–3m troop carriers, which, happily, never arrived! The important thing was to fit bowsprit sails, which pulled the sharp end into wind and acted as automatic steering gear. These ships gave us much pleasure but care had to be taken to avoid the detail getting wet and melting the animal glue!

Rex and I had bought up a big supply of glue from Woolworths because we feared a shortage, which never happened. Later on the full size 'Mosquito' aircraft would be depending upon some more exotic synthetic glues! I also built a few waterline models of modern British battleships: a 'King George V', 'Tribal' and 'J' class destroyers. I even thought of making these to order and put a small glass case on a strut by the front gate of '22I'. Dad was much against this – I think on the grounds it would put the house liable as business premises – overlooking the stream of insurance contributors who called every Monday to pay their premiums! I think I realised the problem that such handmade objects were very slow to make. Anyhow, 1940 became much too lively for me to persist.

The weekly publication *Modern Wonder* offered drawings and photographs of infantry weapons, presumably to interest potential Local Defence Volunteers (later the Home Guard) and, in miniature. I made a Vickers gun on a tripod mount, Bren etc, which could fit in a matchbox. Today (1996), such models in many scales are available as plastic kits but I doubt the builders get as much satisfaction as I did from scraps of firewood. I put together Kielcraft Spitfire and Hurricane kits, I think about 1s 6d each, in Beddington Park while Mum and Dad went into church; I minded our three bikes. These elastic powered machines taught me of balsa and cement, but I cannot recall any actual flights.

By 1942–3 I was experimenting with making 4mm to the 1ft scale, forward-control lorries in wood, card and clear plastic.

The main problem was solved by finding turned model aircraft wheels, which could be given wire axles and tinplate, folded-up bearings. I obtained manufacturers' drawings, photographs and other drawings, from which I concocted 4mm drawings and text for a modest book. This was typed on the machine given to me by Mum and Dad for my 16th birthday in October 1941. I got decent letters of regret from both Cassell's and Percival Marshall publishers. These related to being so "fully occupied in the production of engineering workshop practice books essential to the war effort". Percival Marshall was uncertain as to public demand in future for a book on this "very specialised class of modelling". Skipping through the manuscript over fifty years later, I think it not a bad effort for a self-taught 17-year-old in wartime!

My workshop was the kitchen table, just above the cutlery drawer, and within reach of some warmth from the stove. I had to clear it all away for meals excepting Sunday teatimes. I would be at Air Training Corps until lunchtime those days, but tea would be in the 'front' room. The most useful substance was cardboard and odd pieces from Wallington Court were welcome. The quality varied and I used stuff of about one-sixteenth for 4mm railway wagon bodies, overlaid with thin post card type material for the planking etc. I also came across an embossed tape, which was sliced into half-millimetre strips as 'metal' strapping. One day, cycling back from the post office to Wallington Court offices, I called into the station bookstall and spotted a tiny orange-cover magazine. This was *The Model Railway Constructor* edited by Ernest Carter and, in the early days, published from Colliers Water Lane, Thornton Heath! This, together with the even tinier *Model Railway News*, edited by J. N. Maskelyne, was most important to me and to many other servicemen away from home. Articles by Michael Longridge, particularly, inspired me to try the 18mm gauge, rather than the Rev Edward Beal's and Trix and Hornby Dublo's 16.5mm.

But, in 1943, anything made of metal, especially wheels, was virtually unobtainable, so it was necessary to concentrate on all above the solebar. To modern railway 'modellers' used to buying even quite esoteric models off the shelf, this wartime tale of shortages must seem incredibly frustrating! Typical of the times was the simple article I wrote for the *Model Railway News* for a 'miniature coal order office' that required only card, and scraps of wood and wire. I joined the RAF shortly after my 18th birthday on 30th October and the article appeared while I was finishing square-bashing at Skegness! It is in the tiny January 1944 edition.

In 1944 the British bombing offensive was at its height and leave was restricted to 36-hour passes. This could get me home half way through a day, for a bath and change of clothing, and perhaps an hour of modelling that day and during the following afternoon. By five o'clock we had tea, Mum packed me up a delicious lardy-cake, all fruit and sugar – how she managed this I do not know – and by 6 pm Dad would be walking up the road with me on the way to King's Cross Station. So was the model making fitted in as part of home life and such a contrast to the hectic work on the Mosquito 'flights' and the earth-shaking roar of a hundred Rolls Royce Merlins coughing into action every night, from ourselves on '109' and the Lancasters of '582' Squadron.

Correspondence with Bert and Maude (Everall) at Ross kept me in touch with the real railway world in practice. Both of them, as 'passenger guards', were seeing more and more of the Great Western system.

At Christmas, a large box would arrive from them containing apples and such other items of food as would travel safely. Undoubtedly, the rations in London were much leaner than for folk in the countryside, where bacon, eggs, cheese etc found ways of reaching local tables! I was quite fortunate because my list of RAF 'postings' took me into the territories of all of the 'Big Four' companies, as the GWR, LMSR, LNER and SR were known. Perhaps the most thrilling occurrence was the 'Cook's tour of the European mainland' immediately at the end of the war in May 1945. The railways over there were an almost unrecognisable tangle of demolished, rusting marshalling yards, for it was at the necks of these sidings where bombing had the most effect in disrupting communications – trapping vast amounts of wagons and locomotives – until follow-up raids would set the ammunition etc in transit on fire. But, in eastern England the lines of the LNER stretched around the bomber stations and the steam trains of khaki coloured 'teak' coaches, and freight moved across the countryside on brightly gleaming rails. This experience, glimpsed through the bomb-aimer's nose position in a Lancaster, showed me just how naturally a model railway could be made to fit into the countryside.

After the very near miss of not becoming an infantryman tipped out upon a Japanese beach, I found myself despatched to the Gold Coast in 1946. From the railway interest point of view, the Gold Coast Railway offered access to an admittedly narrow-gauge line, but with enormous eight-coupled locomotives supplied by Hawthorns Leslie etc. The RAF uniform, one sleeve of the KD tunic bearing my 'LAC' props, in red, plus a few cigarettes in a top pocket, was my sole defence against any hostile natives! I strolled around the railway lines and yards at Accra and interviewed the foreman – the only white man around the place. I took dozens of photographs with a small 'Detrola' camera, made in Detroit, USA, and no doubt sold by some USAAF man earlier. The film was '127' size, with sixteen exposures of around 35mm in size. As the customs man said on my way home, "That's not much of a camera!" By about now, in 1947, it seemed that Churchill was judging the Russian bear to be less of a menace and I, with thousands of other RAF tradesmen, might soon be released. With this happy prospect in mind I wrote to the Superintendent of the Line, Great Western Railway, Paddington, asking for a job on demob!

While on demob leave I dug out the old wooden gate of '221' and set in two new concrete posts and a wrought iron gate. Around the back, Dad and I dismantled the Anderson shelter and I managed to rescue the doorpost on which I had burnt, with a magnifying glass, the date 1940 while watching the dogfights overhead. When the site was cleared there was room for the 8ft by 6ft asbestos and wood shed, with corrugated iron roof, which Dad had managed to buy new. This was to house the main terminal of a 18mm gauge line, the running tracks of which would exit through the shed side and proceed, at about three feet in height, all up the border to the upper surface of the coal shed by the house. The layout within the shed comprised of an L shaped baseboard of softboard on a 2in by 1in frame. The main platforms were double-track, with a crossover to release the engine. There were freight tracks and similar facilities and a small locomotive yard with ash and maintenance pits. It was fully signalled by Edwards Bros, each one arriving in a neat wooden box – as I could afford them! The posts were square in section and very good in appearance.

They were worked by a Romford type lever frame with steel wires passing through one-sixteenth copper tube, well greased. The main points were worked similarly. Levers were grouped in the frame so that soldered rail sections were interlocked in a simple fashion e.g. the point had to be set appropriately before the signal could be pulled 'off'. The track was assembled from fibre sleepers, through which chairs were pushed through holes, and the two legs of the strip from which they were folded were spread out and lightly hammered into place. I kept the point radius at 2ft 6in, but was always apprehensive as to whether the 'King' I had acquired from Chessington would negotiate such curves on 18mm gauge. However, I pressed on and utilized the hardwood 3in by 2in material, from which the shelter bunk beds were made, as track bases outside and mounted on posts driven into the border. Happily, the flowers – cornflowers I remember especially – grew up around them and I set the line level against Dad's bubble-glass. Always I was conscious of pioneering the concept of a gauge as tiny as 18mm outside. Although esoteric glues had been developed during the war, these had not reached 'civvy street'. I decided to drill every sleeper with three holes(!) to take small nails both to secure and, hopefully, prevent the sleepers shrinking and tightening the gauge. Once the rail was slipped into place I soldered Omega copper wire loops at each joint to maintain alignment and carry the 12 volts DC current. While so engaged I was observed by Joyce's (girl next door!) boyfriend, a physicist, who asked via my parents as to how a short circuit would be avoided once the rolling stock was put on the track. I conveyed the reply that all axles or wheel tyres were insulated one side from the other. This shows how new was the two-rail concept! When all track was in place, probably by late 1948, the entire surfaces were painted with creosote to try and preserve the sleepers as laid. Up at the house end, I had another flat baseboard, about 6ft by 2ft 6in, on which another small terminal was laid out. Then came the great moment, I remember it well, when I took the Dettmar built 'King', which had cost, at £18, a substantial part of my demob gratuity, down to the shed. Almost immediately, one of the driving wheels worked loose and the whole thing locked solid. The 0-6-0 tank engine performed a little better but both motor and pick-ups, although state-of-the-art at the time, were less than satisfactory. I cannot recall whether or not the entire outside run was operated under power, but I recall the Saloon 9005 being fly-shunted by hand –

giving some indication of the possibilities, which would remain a dream.

From the first-hand viewpoint of three years' work in Mr Gilbert Matthews's Rolling Stock Department, I learnt what being a railwayman was about at a quite traumatic time for the senior people – for nationalization would happen from 1st January 1948. While at Paddington, I typed my own lists of non-coaching passenger vans not only of the GWR, but also of the other three companies. These had dimensions, whether end-door loading, gangwayed or not. We had to know about this stock because the local rolling stock distributors could well have had a 'foreign' (i.e.other Big Four) vans in hand while asking Paddington to meet their 'theatrical' requirements for an end-loading scenery vehicle long enough to take the 'flats'. I would get them to have the painted number checked and might then reply, "It's an end-loading 30 footer – you're OK." It might sound strange but, until I left in 1950, our 'desk' had only sketchy stuff on other companies' rolling stock! One day I turned up with models of GWR Super Saloon 9005 and an 0-6-0 tank engine, number 9713, both mounted on a track on a varnished board. This caused much interest and I was taken to the Superintendent of the Line's inner sanctum where Gilbert Matthews presided. He was generous in his praise, saying that '9005' was his favourite vehicle, remarking on the wine cellar built into the floor! He also liked the livery of 'G coat-of-arms W', which passenger tender locomotives carried, but not the tank engines. This was a memorable occasion in the tobacco and engine smoke filled offices at Paddington – leading to the company offering to find me a draughtsman's job at Swindon. Certainly, I would have loved to have been offered some sort of 'traineeship' but I think this was reserved for those whose fathers had held substantial office. Back at home I was in a dilemma – I already travelled about one hour each way to Paddington, but then I was **home**. Only a serviceman who has spent four Christmases away from home realises what one misses. I did not really relish being in lodgings at Swindon all week. Some of the London clerks did live elsewhere, and I recall 'Taff', who returned to Porthcawl at weekends with the standing joke to him not to forget to lower the steel mesh over the windows lest the 'natives' got him!

Other matters began to take over my spare time. I was studying for the examinations of the Institute of Transport from Paddington and although I enjoyed the job of being a small cog in the Great Western Railway, I was becoming concerned that promotion was going to be exceedingly **slow**. In fact, it was plainly a matter of hanging on for jobs as others retired. Downstairs, on the 'lawn' – the concrete apron between the Royal Hotel and the stop-blocks– saw a continuous flow of us clerks to see the 'foreign' engines from the LMS, LNER and SR, which were tried out on GWR lines in the spring of 1948. I photographed the LMS non-streamlined 'City of Bradford' No. 46236, the LNER A4 streamliners No. 22 'Mallard' and No. 60033 'Seagull', and the SR Bulleid Pacific 35019 'French Line – CGT'. The latter had an LMS tender – no doubt to pick up water en route. The Southern had no water troughs, so no need for tenders with pick-ups.

We also saw a variety of experimental liveries: a 'King' in Caledonian Railway blue; black painted mixed traffic locos with buff lining and also, I seem to recall, a pale, rather insipid, green. Coaches appeared in 'blood and custard' livery. There was a design competition for which I submitted a Pullman style livery but this was found by the panel to be too conventional. The search for a new image was on. At Euston the largely LMS officers were devising 'standard' locos for all Regions. Also the Brown Boveri Swiss gas turbine locomotive made many visits to Paddington, accompanied by the all-pervading smell of hot kerosene.

The amount of paper movement from the Railway Executive seemed to intensify and the writing was plainly on the wall for the cessation of all things associated with the old Big Four organisation. Standardization would prevail. The importance of individual jobs would somehow shrink. The only way a picture for posterity could be created was to do as much as possible by modelling 'in Miniature'. Thus I began to develop the concept – there should be representative trains, passenger and freight, of the Big Four companies as they existed up to the end of December 1947.

There would also be some attempt to represent the 120 separate companies which were drawn together in the 1923 Grouping into the Big Four. This would be limited in terms of complete trains, but it would be good to have at least a single example of each livery, which had since vanished. A 'special' or Royal train would exemplify rail travel at its very best and trains specific to the immense contribution made in both World Wars would be essential. Clearly, there was need for a realistic 'historical' framework for the track: signalling, buildings etc, in which the trains and development over many years could be set. Perhaps, what might be seen as the 'middle ages' of the railways in Britain would be sensible in engineering terms, from late Victorian times (1880s) until 1947.

CHAPTER TWO

The Post-War Era:
1950-1976

By 1950, several matters came together. I was 'going out', as they say, with Mary and the prospects of ever being able to be married and get a mortgage on my railway pay of about £300 per year were remote. Hence, when Gerald Blake suggested I apply for a Personnel job in the London Division of the Generating Board – I simply had to leave what was then Western Region, British Railways. I had become quite disillusioned with the railways' rolling stock building policy – too much first class and the lack of competitive fares for third class passengers – which was resulting in a virtual wipeout situation in London by the operators of Victoria Coach Station. Indeed, my interests turned from rail to road with a new Ross Ensign camera with which I began to photograph PSVs (public service vehicles i.e. buses and coaches) on a considerable scale. Together with Rex Nicholls, who lived nearby, we formed 'Aviation and Transport Photographs', and processed his aircraft negatives and my PSVs. From these we produced prints in his spare 8ft by 6ft bedroom converted to a darkroom. Unfortunately, it was heavily labour-intensive and although we had many enthusiasts as customers, for whom I had a most detailed 'list' available, it would never be a moneymaking business!

I continued to make a small number of railway models and used the tiny amount of axlebox castings etc, which were available from the London shops to which my work gave me access. The fibre sleepers in the garden were, inevitably, shrinking and pulling the 18mm gauge significantly tighter. But these were hectic years. Mary and I visited the Festival of Britain site in 195l, and would marry in 1952.

In the mid–50s, Miss Muriel Groves, with whom I worked, suggested the rather brilliant title of 'Railways in Miniature Museum' – 'RiMM' for short. That title and her abiding interest (her presence at exhibitions etc), continued until her death in 2001.

Not surprisingly, modelling took a back seat as do-it-yourself improvements to No. 55 Keston Road, in our early married years, took priority. The empty front room became an occasional studio in which I photographed local people. Serena was born in 1957 and her pram, a nearly new Silver Cross, was thoroughly overhauled in the 'shops' in my shed. Notwithstanding all these diversions, attention was given to recording the railway models in a Black Book. This noted the company and general description of the model, plus date made. Later on, when security became a potential problem, all stock was marked with our then post code in addition to a number R1, R2 *et seq*. The recording scheme was developed to provide a 5in by 3in card for each vehicle, building, signal box etc. These are kept in Big Four grouping order, giving the references used in the modelling and with an 8mm sticky disc on each card and the underside of the model. This is a system to help future curators of the models to form trains appropriately. The discs are colour coded as follows:

	Paint Date	
Pink	1880–1890	
Gold	1891–1900	
Blue	1901–1913	
Yellow	1914–1922	World War I to grouping
Green	1923–1938	Big Four Grouping to pre WWII
Red	1939–1947	World War II to nationalization

In addition, there is a black ink indication for 'F' for freight or 'P' for passenger train on the disc. This gives some guidance to avoid, for example, unfitted brakes and non-brake piped goods vans being added to passenger trains. Note that although the **building** date of the stock is included on the cards, this might not accord with the date of **painting** shown on the model e.g. a LNWR van of 1916 might be finished as it looked when operated by the LMS in World War II. The appropriate paint date is included on each card as PD, say, 1945. The general scheme, housed in two small box files, has proved effective for thirty years excepting that there are now (1997) two Black Books noting 'R 349' as the latest model.

13

The year of 1959 was of great significance in the small railway modelling field for it was then that Hornby Dublo produced **two-rail** track on a plastic base, with new locomotives and rolling stock having insulated wheels. I remember the Christmas, when as any small boy might (although I was thirty-four years old!), Mary and my parents walked up the stairs of the largest Worthing Department Store to the toy floor. There I purchased a Hornby Dublo set comprising Southern 0-6-0 tank engine and a few wagons, with an oval of the new track. This gave me considerable food for thought, posing the inevitable problem – to try and struggle on with the 18mm gauge or to change back to the 16.5mm of the old pioneers with much neater wheel standards. I had already sensed that workers in 18mm plus gauges were into problems of clearances, particularly for pony trucks, valve gear etc, and only the simplest of layouts seemed to be operational at the time. Visually, the difference in the track gauge appeared minimal, except when stock was viewed end-on and most were seen 3/4 front or sideways – where the difference seemed immaterial. In later years, when showing the models at Fairfield Hall and other venues, only the really keen enthusiasts would ask whether the models were 16.5 or 18mm. It appeared to have minimal significance as all distances compared with the real thing, for example station layouts, simply **have** to be compressed in modelled form. My other consideration was strictly practical – the maintenance of models for public display, where something is always **expected** to be operational (and some people will have travelled some distance to see a catalogued item) which in turn would put a great strain on locomotives built as precisely as possible with scale size valve gear etc. I could not see manufacturers catering widely for anything other than 16.5mm gauge in ready-to-run locomotives and stock. I figured that to have engines with Hornby or Trix, new two-rail wheels and mechanisms would ensure pick-ups which were reliable and power 'units' which could be simply be taken out and **replaced** within hours in an operating museum situation.

Hence, a basic eight-coupled Dublo mechanism with appropriate wheelbase and wheel diameter could have several uses and, indeed, does on RiMM. I had kept in touch with Roye England, founder of Pendon Museum near Didcot. He would persist with 18mm gauge and had attracted sufficient skilled model engineers to work to very fine standards. Although my overall aim for

RiMM became quite well known, such modellers as could work to 'Pendon' standards were indeed few – I reckoned perhaps two in the societies local to Croydon. In the event, single-handed compilation of RiMM enabled me to set a scheme which would particularly compensate for the absence of certain significant items from full size preservation. Bear in mind that in 1960 hardly anything other than some Royal Train items had survived!

I decided to reproduce some compound locomotives which did not deserve to be discarded, but developed as on mainland Europe; so the North Eastern Smith Atlantic and the LNWR Webb compound 'Victoria and Albert' were built. The Atlantic wheelbase, of American origins, was also important in British locomotive development and a Lancashire & Yorkshire 'Highflyer' is included, together with a GCR 'Jersey Lily'. Four-coupled, 4-4-0 engines are also represented: the SECR 'E' Class on the 1914 Royal Train, a T6 on the LSWR train to the west, and a Southern Railway 'Schools' – 'Stowe'. Superheating of the steam was an important stage in engine development and the Caledonian Railway 'Cardean' is a famous engine which probably represented the peak of express design in the non-superheated era. The L & Y 'Highflyer' is noted as the first superheated express locomotive in Britain and the SECR 'E' is shown with the Schmidt version fitted in 1912. The range of RiMM, from the GWR single-wheeler 'Duke of Connaught', through four and six-coupled tank engines, 4-6-0s, to the 'Pacifics' of the LMS, LNER and SR, illustrate development of British railways in a most compact form, from 1880 to 1947. I hope that those who come after me will respect that I have done my best to apply my 'spare' time to this task. I have had to earn my living otherwise!

Not surprisingly, in view of my involvement with non-passenger carrying, passenger rated (charged) stock on the GWR; I felt this area and that of special freight wagons to be little known and under-represented in full size preservation and historical modelling. As and when drawings and photographs came to hand, I tried to make such models – and still do! It is well known that coal and other minerals provided the greatest revenue for most railways but they were, until the Transport Act 1962, required to act as common carriers of everything from plate-glass to elephants! The variety of Special Freight rolling stock and the equally varied loads constitute a substantial proportion

15

of the RiMM exhibits and it is pleasing to see that this fascination seems to be shared by young and old.

The 'Black Book' shows a survey of building in 1960 – undoubtedly, inspired by the Hornby Dublo track. I also 'itched' to get something actually running and turned the front room at 55 Keston Road into a model railway around the furniture! Basically, a baseboard about 2ft 6in by 6ft would support a considerably compressed version of Ross-on-Wye Station, yards and buildings. The buildings were drawn from photographs and some measurements I took while the family was on holiday. Around the room, brackets screwed into the walls supported plywood track bases with a section of embankment and fencing. The curved sections were supported on three-eighths by one-eighth soft iron strip on edge, set apart about four inches by metal tube distant pieces, over which ERG curved track bases were fixed. A wooden canopy covered the Ross Station area, with plastic sheet over this and the rest of the layout, in strips, to keep the dust at bay. Certainly, the running was quite reliable upon a mixture of Peco and Hornby track. It took from 1961 to 1965 to build. S W (Steve) Stevens-Stratten, editor of the *Model Railway Constructor* and I had corresponded earlier while I was stationed in Africa. Now he paid a visit and was quite shocked when an eight-coupled 28XX backed out of Ross engine shed – an early example of bodywork by me upon a Hornby chassis. He published many of my drawings and photographs of the Ross buildings, this record being largely responsible for the recreation of the Kidderminster terminal on the Severn Valley Railway!

In 1962 our Susan Ann was born and the family was complete. I converted the small upstairs darkroom back into its rightful role – as a bedroom. Another nearly new Silver Cross received a full overhaul and went 'into traffic'!

The years from 1963 to 1967 seem particularly productive and the Black Book records many models. This was the period when many ex-chief officers of the Big Four, Croydon Corporation, and Gulbenkian were all contacted with a view to establishing RiMM on some spare ground alongside the railway in South Croydon. A post book for the period is indicative of the efforts made but, as not unusually, the idea of RiMM was before its time. It as not until we had left Croydon in 1985 that the Council converted the old town hall to be a museum, where RiMM might have been accommodated!

Good wishes came in from Sir Malcolm Barclay-Harvey, O. V. S. Bulleid, H G Ivatt, Derby Museum, *Meccano* magazine, *Railway Gazette*, Ministry for Arts, and Sir Harold Hartley, and I will add below a letter personally typed (I'm sure no typist would make so many mistakes!) by John Betjeman, as he then was:

---

43 Cloth Fair,

London E.C.1
March 23rd 1967

Dear Sir,

I am very pleased to have your letter of March 21st. My interest in railways has been more in station architecture and tunnels and viaducts than in engines and rolling stock.

I think the Great Central Sam Fay class with one of those trains from Sheffield to Marylebone in pre-Grouping days would be a joy to see, also the London and South Western Waterloo to Exeter and Padstow expresses. And before it disappears altogether shouldn't we have the Bournemouth Belle, Pullmans and all.

With best wishes,
Yours sincerely,
John Betjeman

Naturally, I was well pleased with his response although no financial support had emerged from any source. Readers are invited to view the RiMM display and note how Sir John's wishes have been interpreted. Christmas 1967 saw us with a display which included a huge walnut showcase I obtained for £3(!) from under the Science Museum! This case was carried by six men up the staircase in the foyer of the newly opened Fairfield Hall, Croydon, and placed in a prominent position in the exhibition space. I actually used steam sound tape recordings I had made at Ross to support the general effect. Visitors included teachers and children on Christmas holidays. The actors and musicians appearing in the shows would often stroll around and look at the trains. I clearly recall David Jason so doing. Overall, I felt, as the accepted 'founder' of the concept, that I must continue efforts to raise the finance needed to fund a permanent display.

Looking back at the productions for 1967, I note the mix of rolling stock emerging from 55 Keston: a World War II Warwell bogie wagon carrying an example of the famous British designed, but United States built 'Sherman' tank; a Great Northern double-bolster wagon with load of tree trunks; a Southern Railway engineers' crane; a 'Mica B' GWR refrigerated van; and an SR 'Crocodile' bogie well wagon conveying a diesel alternator by English Electric – as used for RAF airfield standby power from 1940. While the modelling continued, I realised that no money would be forthcoming for the South Croydon site. The deaths of both Bert Everall and my mother were to make 1968 a most distressing year.

Nevertheless, I rallied and decided to rebuild the wooden shed at the bottom of our garden in the style of a railway signal box, with sliding windows and the cast plate 'Ross Signal Box' from the full size building on the side. I drew up the plans and consulted our neighbour opposite, Fred Stone, an ex-RAF fitter, who earned his living painting and decorating. Fred had renewed most front garden fences and walls locally, and he agreed my design was practicable. In principle, there would be a continuous 'run' for the trains through the model Ross Station, the lines coming out through the side wall on No. 57's side, up the border, around the Cox's tree outside our living room window. It then crossed a bridge over the path, returning above the border against No. 53, and so back under the canopy of the new building, providing a route by which the 'Hereford' trains returned to Ross Station.

The roof of this building was covered with corrugated clear plastic and some insulation sheet to keep the heat down in summer and retain some warmth in winter. Insulation sheet, battened off the breeze blocks, helped insulate the sides and took the painted acrylic backgrounds very well. In all the building cost £210. Fred and I drank a Scotch to celebrate the finished job, with which I think he was as pleased as myself. I did the wiring and the windows were actually free – so many being replaced locally with the new plastic frames. The heaviest job was putting the cast iron nameplate in place – certainly some 1 cwt (50 kg) in weight!

The amount of track laying, in Peco Streamline, both inside and out, wooden supports etc, was to occupy me quite fully between 1970 and 1973. It was quite a palaver to put up the temporary 'bridges' across the path at both ends. Each point had a soldered Omega loop of .029in copper wire and I ran two additional leads from the signal box to the return curve by the Cox's tree, because voltage drop was a factor. At least I can record successful runs by 'Sir Nigel Gresley' and my 'Castle' class 'Sir Daniel Gooch' with three or four coach trains. We were open several days during school holidays and for the St Jude's garden fete. I managed to obtain some surplus plastic guttering, free, from the manufacturer OSMAS changing specification. These sections sat over the outside trackwork and kept the dirty atmosphere and weather off the rails. Although the sleepers were not absorbent, the so-called nickel silver (actually an alloy of nickel, copper and zinc) seemed much affected by the generally polluted atmosphere of Thornton Heath. I had in mind that phosphor-bronze rail section might be better but, even by 1997, I have not tried it in practice.

Mr H. R. Lines, a director of Lines Bros Ltd (Triang), was most hopeful in the supply of various bits and pieces and wrote, in June 1969, that he felt opening the garden museum would provide publicity and 'This will surely be the turning point for you.' This was encouraging but over-optimistic! Some data was pored over regarding a Pullman train, as John Betjeman had suggested, and a variety of Triang coaches, plus some later Hornbys were gradually acquired. A sample book of fade proof fabrics by the Sundour company of the 1930s, rescued from a jumble sale, was to provide excellent upholstery and curtains for the Pullmans, the SECR Royal Train and others. In 1972, a Wainwright 'J' class emerged from the Keston Road 'shops': number 1596 and destined to be the last 0-6-4 tank engine to run on British Rail. A Caledonian open carriage truck followed, with a 1906 Rolls Royce Silver Ghost motor car as load. Both models were handbuilt. For the car I made drawings scaled off a photograph of a 'Lesney' model. A Southern bogie luggage and a four-wheeled covered carriage truck were modified commercial models in 1972. At this time an enthusiast recalls visiting the Norwood Carriage Works in 'Southern' days and finding five different shades of green paint in use at the same time! Consternation among modellers who prefer to see a rigid distinction of time and place in railway liveries – but, the practicalities of what the foreman has to hand usually wins! A Highland motor car van was built with the end doors in the 'open' position and with a bull-nosed Morris car emerging, reflecting the background to the current TV series *Dr Finlay's Casebook*, and much admired by the public.

The New Year, 1973 found me engaged in a quite rare event: the making of a pair of wagons, actually 'Rectanks' – 35 ton load bogie flats for the conveyance of armoured fighting vehicles. One carries a Mk 1 tank returning from France with its six-pounder gun sponsons packed inside to keep within the loading gauge. On the way to the continent this load would have been 'crated', for the War Office wished it known the contents was a 'water' tank, for surprise was to be the essence of the tanks' first use in 1916. The second truck depicts an example bought by the GWR between the wars and now in World War II, conveying a Bren gun ('Universal') carrier and a six-pounder anti-tank gun. Between February and July 1973 I engaged in something of a marathon – the construction of three GWR coaches of 1926 vintage, with sides painfully drilled and filed out from Boots talcum powder tins! I did send a photograph to Boots and although admired, they would offer no financial support for RiMM. Another half-dozen models occupied the rest of the year including, over three months, a Lancashire & Yorkshire 'Highflyer' upon one of three dismantled 4-6-2 chassis acquired from Trix. A photograph in *Kitchener's Army*, by the author/journalist Edgar Wallace, depicted a 13-pounder field gun on a 25ft 6in wagon chassis. Library research helped with the detail added to an Airfix kit of the gun. A Midland Railway bogie snowplough enabled a modern day recyclement following on the MR's own use of a surplus single-wheeler's tender. I had a spare LNER A4 tender which was similarly rebuilt.

In 1974 I realised that the collection was, due to modelling the Ross-on-Wye location, entirely biased towards GWR signalling practice. Accordingly, I began to sort out some drawings and photographs of other companies, both pre-1923 Grouping and afterwards. An LNWR and a Lancashire & Yorkshire example was made and this opened the door for me to an interesting, special aspect of railway operations. Having several Triang point motors in hand, which I considered somewhat underpowered as such, I modified them to work the signals remotely. The basic idea emerging was to position a signal of the same company at the exit of the siding in which an appropriate train is normally stored within the museum setting. The year 1974 saw another locomotive under construction, the handsome Smith Compound 'Atlantic' No. 730, upon a reduced Trix A3 chassis. Real gold dust was applied to the North Eastern coat-of-arms on the tender – a beautiful design of engine which might have been much replicated if it were not for patent problems. A couple of horse boxes, one short, one long wheelbase of LSWR origin followed in 1975, as did engine No. 265: a 'Jersey Lily' 'Atlantic' of 1904, again incorporating a modified Trix chassis.

When I left CEGB Research Headquarters at Paternoster the previous year, I had as a present six Roxey Moulding kits depicting LSWR coaches of the turn of the century. At my leaving presentation I showed a completed coach model and gave the assembly a short lecture (!) on RiMM and its purpose. I think the reaction of the largely scientific audience was, to use a current phrase, somewhat 'gobsmacked', which was my intention, to deflate considerable humbug. The building and fitting out of this stock with 'Sundour' fabrics upholstery and curtains occupied most of 1975 but I was most pleased with the result, especially, perhaps, the oil painted coats-of-arms.

A conscious effort was made, in 1976, to examine the tank wagons represented and to add to the milk and oil tankers a bogie chlorine tanker, Redline and Ensign petrol, seed crushers (margarine oil) and Yorkshire tar! Schoolchildren always view this stock with incredulity – this I conclude is due to them imagining that a wagon might carry tar one day and milk the next! Three Hornby Dublo non-corridor coaches were seen as closely matching the 59ft Bulleid Southern stock of 1945 and a set was duly detailed. As is my usual practice, one brake is fitted with pick-ups on the bogies, which end in phosphor bronze sprung 'sockets' next to the engine. Each locomotive has two flexible extensions out through the tender (or bunker), which terminate in 14mm 'Duchess' dressmaking pins soldered on. These simply plug into the van end. The idea is to provide an extra source of traction pick-up for the engines and also, where fitted, the coach lighting.

Looking at the miniature Ross goods yard, I saw the need for some coal wagons and realised the Forest of Dean was losing its pits, so that recording the liveries was historically worthwhile. In 1976 I constructed a Princess Royal Colliery of Whitecroft wagon, a Northern H Crawshaw of Cinderford, Cannop Colliery of Speech House Road, and New Bowson of Cinderford. These would be static exhibits in Ross coal yard and fitted with 3-link couplings. This brings me to the couplings in use in RiMM generally. As long ago as the 1940s, I found by experiment that the relatively sharp radius curves we modellers are forced to use, make strictly full size practice almost impossible. Even short wagons would quickly buffer-lock and derail. Long wheelbase four and six-wheeler vans were very difficult – as indeed Hornby and Triang were well aware. The problems with bogie-stock become worse with increasing length i.e. equivalent to 70ft full size.

Essentially, the bogie problem can be solved if the coupling is connected to the bogie frame and not the solebar, which swings out substantially even on 3ft radius curves in 00 scale. The best commercial system seemed to be the 'knuckle' coupling of Hornby Dublo and this I developed slightly, by increasing slightly the size of the actual hook and not fitting the downward extension for remote uncoupling. These I draw out on ex-electric fire reflector material – chromed brass – for which I made a pattern. Others are simply drawn around, with the pivot point varied to suit buffer length of each wagon, and folded up. This has become the standard for freight stock; but, not for one end of each brake van, which carries the tail lamp and has correct coupling according to prototype.

For coaching stock which had knuckle-coupling, then RiMM does so likewise. Where a screw-coupling was fitted, then either a hole or a 4mm vertical length of one-sixteenth diameter brass tube is fitted. Into these drops a length of .029in copper wire, bent to an 'M' shape. This is bound with a cosmetic braid of fuse wire and so resembles vacuum pipe. Across the top of the M shape is a wire made 'screw-coupling', soldered to the vertical .029. These are of several different overall sizes, dependent on the length of coaches being coupled. Sharp eyed boys at exhibitions remark favourably on this scheme, which is particularly suited to stock following full size practice and being normally operated in 'sets'. As with the coal wagons at Ross, all vehicles built for static display have correct couplings, vacuum or Westinghouse and steam heating hoses.

The year 1976 continued to be productive and an LMS cattle truck, LNER Implement, Great Eastern machine wagon with a threshing machine and a portable steam engine as loads appeared. An LMS special cattle van passenger train rated; an LNER (ex-North Eastern) snowplough and a Great Central Railway refrigerator van completed a busy mixture.

CHAPTER THREE

The RiMM Collection
from 1977

In 1977, I spotted an unusual combination depicted in Pratt's *British Railways in the Great War*. This was an ex-Naval 8in gun which Swindon Works had mounted as a howitzer for field use and carried on an unfinished 'Open A' – reflecting the gun's urgent need at the front. This photograph was duly converted into a '3-D' model and the year included a Great Eastern loco coal, North Staffordshire goods brake, North British bogie bolster, Midland & Great Northern gas tank wagon for coach lighting, Metropolitan goods van with loco pick-ups, Midland and South West junction furniture flat with a pantechnicon and a GWR crocodile bogie-well wagon with excavator load... Never let it be said that RiMM was anything but Catholic in taste! I then turned to coaching stock and produced a Great Eastern lavatory luggage first/third composite. Four Dublo LNER coaches were converted backwards in time to appear in the rich crimson livery of the North Eastern railway: a very smart train behind the green Smith 'Atlantic'.

In April the writer noted the York Museum were intending to expand their model railway exhibition and I wrote to Roye England at Pendon and also to York. I cannot recall whether York ever deigned to reply to me, but Roye certainly did and I reproduce below what he wrote in his tiny, careful writing:

c/o 4 Tatlings Road,
Steventon, Abingdon,
Oxon.
3rd July, 1977

Dear Eric,

I was very pleased to hear from you again, and to know that RiMM is still going ahead well. I think you are very brave to undertake such a work single-handed, but you have obviously covered a great deal of ground in your limited spare time over the years, and when you reach the happy time of retirement you should really make progress. I attained that state of bliss some years ago, and it has made an incredible difference to what I can do.

At the moment, however, I am in rather low gear, as I had a cataract operation three months ago and have still not got the lens or glasses that I now need. That happened before you wrote and is the reason for my very delayed reply. Writing at first became very difficult, and though I've got more used to it since then, it is still an effort. It will apparently be another three weeks or so before I am properly fixed up – and I'm chafing to get back to modelling.

All goes very well at Pendon, the only exception being a disaster to our lighted train, in which 'River Plym' with four coaches and a bogie van plunged five feet to the concrete floor. It was no-one's fault and we can't account for how it happened, unless possibly, it was due to buffer locking after one of the coaches had been attended to. The damage is extensive and is a real setback. However, in other ways progress is quite encouraging, so it could be worse.

You say you hope to be holidaying later in the year and that you may be able to get to Pendon. I do hope so, and that I shall be at the museum when you come. I am not living there now, as there were so many interruptions with phone calls and people coming even when we were not open, that I was getting nowhere fast. So I have come to live with friends at Steventon, eight miles from Pendon, and I go there most Saturdays but not so often on Sundays.

Must stop now, with very best wishes for your project – and thanks for your mention of Pendon to the NRM.

Sincerely,
Roye England

Sad to relate, I never made it to Pendon, but I was then extremely involved with my job as Personnel Officer to five Southwark Council departments in 1977. I continued to keep in touch with Pendon and eventually one of my contacts told me that Roye was really ill and if I ever wanted to see him, the time was then. He slipped away with much of what he wished to see achieved – he had climbed such a steep slope to the success he and his close modellers created.

A curious set of circumstances was waiting around the corner of the New Year, 1978, and this had all started way back in 1967, at one of the every second-year appearances of the RiMM stand at Fairfield Hall, Croydon. Having set up everything I turned to face an elderly gentleman emerging from the lift near our stand. Says he, "I was the driver of the train that took the Empress of all the Russias and staff from London to Dover on 1st August 1914, the day World War I began! Here are the secret working papers I risked my job to keep." This was indeed a very special happening. I took the instructions from him, printed on pink paper to indicate their importance. Driver W. Barton was in a wheelchair now, but he really enjoyed talking to me. The Special Instructions detailed engine No. 275, two Royal brake saloons, a corridor first, a first saloon lavatory and '1R' – King Edward VII's saloon with 'Royal' clerestory roof and crown symbols on sides.

The references in *Carriage Stock of the SECR* by David Gould and the Historical Model Railway Society drawings were to be essential. The upshot of this meeting at Fairfield was that I promised to make the rolling stock and locomotive. Driver Barton was very happy to leave the instructions with me. As it happens, it took me eleven years before I made the coaches and 1979 before the engine, with rocking inside valve gear and full Royal flags, Russian Double Eagle, Tricolour and Ensign on the smokebox, was completed. Needless to say, the Sundour fabrics grace the carriage interiors and the Empress and her suite were dressed in the pastel colours so fashionable in London in the last peacetime summer until 1919.

While at Fairfield Hall, David Jenkinson, then Research Head, National Railway Museum, York, was deputed by the Office of Arts and Libraries to visit RiMM and make an assessment of the project. I set below the gist of the Department's response, dated 10th October 1979:

Following his visit to the 'Railways in Miniature' stand at the Fairfield Halls in June, Mr Jenkinson reported very favourably on the inherent interest and quality of your collection. As you will appreciate, we are not in a position to promise any material support for your planned permanent display, since this will be essentially a local venture; but we would certainly support your objectives in principle and wish you every success in achieving them.

Yours sincerely,
Mrs S. G. EVANS
for the Office of Arts and Libraries

This was most welcome although not entirely surprising, as I was able to talk to David Jenkinson as a fellow mature person, who had studied railways with equal depth and interest as myself. Although finance would have been welcome, I consoled myself in the belief that if something is sufficiently worth it – the necessary accommodation and funding will **eventually** happen! By 1980, I was fifty-five years of age and had in mind retiring at sixty, to Ross, where all the dreams might come true: a practical thought being that Ross certainly represented a Middle-England location

– between the Science Museum in London and the Railway version at York! Again, I turned to the gaps in the collection and, between February and September, constructed the 'Alfred the Great' class compound made in the time of Frances Webb on the LNWR. Bearing a huge nameplate 'Victoria and Albert', the rivet-encrusted product of Crewe shops has austere lines and is such a contrast to the smooth recessed rivet finish of the Ashford works 4-4-0 on the Royal Train. Happily, Ratio had kits for appropriate LNWR bogie coaches dating from the turn of the century. These are fitted with Jackson metal wheels and the fitted interiors are electrically lit. Four 3 volt bulbs are wired in series in each coach. Phosphor bronze sockets engage with 14mm pin 'plugs' wired between the carriages. One of the problems is that something over 1.5 amps is taken when an engine is pulling a rake of lit coaches – and this is just about when the current limiter on power packs cuts in! However, they can be switched off at the front brake and it is a nice feature for occasional use.

It might be mentioned that it is a principle with RiMM to provide a good presence of appropriately finished passengers in the coaches. As far as practicable, for most are painted figures from Slater's range, the people are matt finished in the largely dull shades of the 1880–1947 period. No census has yet been held (by 1997!) but there must be over a thousand passengers, many of which were painted by my daughter, Serena, in her teens. The LNWR work occupied me until December 1980, when I became fascinated by the photograph of a 1906 LCC 'F' class tramcar – a single-decker and the first electric car in north London. A search of the HMRS lists revealed an LNWR tramcar trolley fitted with rails to accommodate three gauges: 4ft 8½in, 4ft and 3ft 6in, of trams. I made a drawing of the tram from the photograph, and it and the trolley wagon were both built in the Keston Road 'shops'. Later, at a Fairfield showing, a keen road vehicle enthusiast asked to photograph this little cameo for publication, declaring that he had never before seen a model of an 'F' class tram. This experience does tend to happen because most modellers will not attempt to make a model if a drawing or a kit cannot be found.

In parallel with the LNWR work in 1980, I carried out some research into the LNER ambulance trains of World War II. Both the SR and the LNER *Railways at War* booklets revealed some details, as did contemporary copies of the *MRN* and *Railway*

Magazine, although this was a distinctly secret area in wartime. Nevertheless, I found sufficient information to be able to compile the 'Knight Errant' ambulance train formation, first from Hornby stock, converting (as had the real railway companies!) a sleeping car to include a dining 'mess' section. All underframes were replaced. Two Ian Kirk vehicles were added (in 1984) as ward cars, to complete a seven-coach train. The appropriate engine, a B 12/3 4-6-0, was an ex-Great Eastern Holden design, rebuilt by Gresley in 1932 and by Thompson in 1943 with a new boiler etc. Yes, economy was the name of the game! Fortunately, Hornby had made a model in the rebuilt form, to which I added shuttered side windows, rolled blackout sheet etc. With all the coaches in khaki drab and red crosses on a white background on sides and roof, the sight of this train jolts one back to the time immediately before the invasion of Europe in June 1944. Happily, such trains were less used than those which served the injured from the trench warfare of 1914–18. Indeed, some identical coaches served in both World Wars and provided comfortable facilities entirely beyond road transport capability.

The New Year of 1981 found me back to World War I and a six-wheel aero truck of the LSWR. The load was a French 'Spad' fighter built under licence in the UK, and finished in 1917 high-gloss dope; an Airfix kit. Another HMRS drawing enabled construction of an LSWR bogie open carriage truck of 1904, as used for a variety of fast transits on passenger trains – the load being sheeted scenery 'theatricals' with property baskets and in this case with a pantechnicon.

Theatrical companies would move by passenger train on Sundays, having given a 'last night' performance on the Saturday in one town and opening at a new location on Monday evening! What stamina those stage folk had – how often as they waited to 'go on' their tired brains must have tried desperately to remember **where** they actually were! This traffic was quite intense – valuable to the railways – certainly up to 1950 when it was a regular weekly task for the GWR's passenger desk (at Paddington) to see that the right vehicles were in place by Saturday all over the system. I can't think of a single case of failure to 'supply' in time.

Making this vehicle reminded me of the Great Western's 'Jumbo' van, a 28ft 6in Covered Carriage Truck, coded 'Python A'. This van, No. 580, was the only one on the line strengthened with three-eighths of an inch steel plates on floor and sides to counter an elephant's natural tendency to kick its way out of a container! The full size vehicle was often used by Bertram Mills circus – one brother was especially knowledgeable and he would specify the running numbers of the vehicles he wanted in the circus train. I built No. 580 with the end doors open so that an elephant could be shown in process of loading. This first appeared at Fairfield Hall in May 1981. My good wife, Mary, modelled the animal in plasticine, which was sealed and varnished, then painted elephant grey. Such 'life' modelling is quite beyond me, but most effective and appealing to the children and their parents!

In the autumn I turned my attention to four Hornby GWR coaches, two corridor composites 'Cricket Cs' and two brake thirds 'Melon Bs' in the telegraph code lingo. These were fitted with 3 volt bulbs (four to each vehicle), upholstered seating, mirrors and photographs on the partitions. The underframes were detailed with dynamos etc, and the bogies replaced by BSL castings of GWR pattern.

Next year, 1982, the pendulum swung to the LMS and some modifications to two Hornby corridor brake thirds, and a 60ft first/third composite by Airfix/Mainline. Similar detailing to the GW stock took place, including interior lighting. I also acquired a Hornby 6-wheeled gangwayed passenger brake van and a bogie covered carriage truck by Lima – both good models, detailed with the aid of Essery drawings. A covered combination truck (CCT) of 1934, for the carriage of motor cars and scenery 'flats', was built, and incorporated some Hornby six-wheeled components from the Palethorpes' van. The basic engineering of this chassis was quite a revelation, incorporating a mechanism to slide the centre set of wheels to accommodate the sharp Dublo curves. I used some light aluminium springy strips under the movable centre section so that it might 'float' in running. The rather heavy rods attached to the Triang type couplings were removed since I use the HD knuckle-type.

Two 'open' fitted trucks followed. A four-wheeler of 1939, plainly designed by the LMS in anticipation of the war, carries an AEC Matador artillery tug. The six-wheeled prototype road-railer has two insulated tankers for milk, all built by myself. The most interesting feature, and probably the Achilles heel of the whole idea, was the 16(!) screw couplings needed to secure the road tankers at every end loading – twice every day. I use the word 'prototype' in the sense used in the aircraft world – meaning an experimental full size item; for some unknown reason the model railway fraternity, but **not** real railwaymen, always call any full size object the 'prototype'.

In 1982 I tried to find out about the horse-drawn fire engine which served Ross from 1899 to 1927! Enquiries, including to the press and local historian Fred Druce, Monmouth Museum etc, all drew blanks. The engine appeared in a few photographs, but much obscured by firemen on and around it. My best source was the Science Museum where a full size example exists. One of the keepers kindly crawled over it for me and filled in a questionnaire giving dimensions needed. This, together with an excellent photograph, enabled a fascinating model to be built and shown as if 'on delivery' to Ross on a GWR 'Loriot' well wagon of 1890 vintage. I constructed another batch of passenger-rated vehicles this year, all six-wheelers, using cut-up Horby chassis. These comprised a North British covered carriage truck No. 69, a Rhymney Railway version, a Glasgow & South Western luggage brake using some commercial mouldings, and a London & South Western special milk van. The latter, for conveyance of milk in churns, has a complicated slatted body to facilitate the flow of air and keep the milk cool.

January 1983 saw a GW 'Loriot P' in World War II use, conveying a British armoured personnel carrier/artillery tug and an LNER 'Mac NV' loaded with a 25-pounder gun. In February I acquired an Airfix/GMR, LMS 0-6-0 goods engine, of which seven hundred and fifty were in use during the Second War; this was detailed including the blackout sheet between locomotive and tender. In considerable contrast was an SR 'Schools' class 'Stowe' to represent probably the most powerful 3-cylinder 4-4-0s built. A Hornby model (reminding me of their 'O' version) was obtained, with added detail and a headcode as 'No. 10 Special Boat Train Waterloo–Southampton'. This engine simply called out for a train of Pullmans, as Sir John Betjeman had suggested long before.

The vehicles owned by the Pullman Car Company were leased to many British railway companies over the years, including South Eastern & Chatham, LNER, GWR (very briefly), Metropolitan, SR, Midland, LBSC, GNR, and Caledonian. After the Grouping, with the exception of the GWR in 1925, only the Southern and the London & North Eastern leased cars. The entire *raison d'etre* for the Pullman Car was to provide comfortable accommodation for those accustomed to the best class of hotel, shipping and air travel. It follows that the hired stock was subject to frequent internal refurbishment, renewal, cleaning etc, and this included some quite drastic rebuilding e.g. to add or remove a kitchen, and changes of seating to upgrade or downgrade the vehicle class. Traditionally, the first class cars bore names, usually female in gender, but quite often having some contemporary relevance to the times, as 'Iolanthe' and 'Arcadia'. The second and third class cars were numbered only. Over the years 1874 to 1947, some quite exotic combinations of wood panelling, curtaining and carpeting appeared, with upholstery including silk damask and calf leather. Each car, in a lifetime of perhaps forty years, could have appeared in four or more distinct roles and the subject can only be representatively shown in RiMM.

All the RiMM Pullmans are finished in the 'new' standard livery from 1929 to 1942 (war break ran from 1945 to 1958) being umber fascia boards under cantrail and below waist with cream between. This glamorous world is represented by the first class car 'Agatha' of 1928 with a paint date of 1946, the name being connected with the writer Agatha Christie. 'Sapphire' is a first class car rehabilitated after World War II service as a NAAFI refreshment car. Originally built in 1910 and worked by the SE & CR, 'Camilla' is also shown as a 1946 rebuild, having served the Metropolitan Railway both as a kitchen car and composite from 1932. Car No. 30 is third class, with Southern Railway No. 2 gauge restriction as in 1927; previously No. 18 and second class in 1922! Two third class corridor parlour brakes appear as in 1946: No.s 78 and 80. The former ran earlier in the 'Queen of Scots' Pullman set. Sir John, I hope you look down with some joy on these 'Sundour' upholstered lovelies!

The New Year, 1984 was rather special to me as in my long-term plan, I saw it as my last full year working in London. I would be sixty years old and hoped to retire early. As I looked at the collection of some two hundred models, the matter of dismantling the 'signal box' layout, contents, sorting and packing the rest stored in our bedroom and the front room cupboard was a weighty task. Mary collected many strong cardboard boxes, biscuit tins etc, and I packed the models 'by company' in order

A model of the original design for a Museum at South Croydon, alongside the Southern East Croydon–Brighton main line. The full size Great Western Saloon was allocated to 'RiMM' until Swindon Council objected. 1967.

The Founder, age 72 years, in the process of cutting out panelling and windows for the Great Central Railway coaches, pre-1914 war. 1998.

Ross Station, Hereford; passenger train about to depart, the loading of circus elephants and the arrival from a covered carriage truck of Dr. Finlay's bull-nosed Morris car. The large water tank represents the perimeter of Ross Station area.

Ross Station; auto-train about to depart for Monmouth from Bay Platform. Behind the signal box are numerous visiting trains including LSWR. and Southern 'Schools' with Pullman cars. In the distance stands the Gartside Viaduct and the Post Windmill.

to give some order to locating particular items when the great **un**packing at Ross became possible. This has not yet happened as I write in 1996!

CHAPTER FOUR

Preparations to Leave London:
1984

In retrospect, the 1984 packing programme alone seemed a pretty awesome task, but the Black Book reveals a full and Catholic 'mix' of new rolling stock. Three vehicles appeared representing the LNER: a 'Protrol E' well wagon with a marine propellor as load, and two 'Toad D' goods brake vans. For the Great Central there was a twin-bolster with tram pylons load, and an extended sided open truck of 1908; the latter believed to be an experiment to combat the van shortage at the time. A Hornby Hull & Barnsley goods van was a rare type for a commercial model and to which I added new ventilators etc. One of the oft ignored features of non-mineral carrying open wagons was the fact that the goods carried were usually 'sheeted' with tarpaulins to protect the contents from weather and to deter theft. A burst of activity in this area followed, adding LSWR, Southern, Barry and Taff Vale railway examples to RiMM.

An unusual private owner van lettered 'Robert Hutchinson & Co' is a rebuilt Triang peaked roof design called a 'grain van'. It appears to have roof-only doors and I speculate that the loads were bottled products - put in and out by crane for security! A Nick Campling drawing inspired a North Eastern 45ft bogie covered carriage truck of 1915, which I built and loaded with two early motor cars which would have been driven in through the end doors. A six-wheel Caledonian horse box, with central groom's compartment, was an interesting bit of coach craft for which I made a drawing from a single photograph. Also in 1984 I was attracted to the excellent models of GWR gangwayed bogie milk vans by Mainline and Lima. Earlier, actually in 1960, I had rebuilt with card body a Dublo coach as a Siphon G PN 1453. I unearthed this vehicle from store and found the comparison most interesting. Undoubtedly, twenty-four years(!)on, the plastic mouldings were so much better, but I decided to retain '1453' in the collection as an example of how the hobby has developed. A 'Siphon H' end-loading scenery van, by Mainline, acquired new 'American' 9ft bogies, gas tanks for lighting etc. This last full year at 55 Keston Road saw attention given to a number of locomotives purchased over the years. An SR 'Battle of Britain' air-smooth 'Pacific' by Hornby was described by me as "beautiful as it is". However, I added headcode No 9, Waterloo–Plymouth – my rough notes are a page long of added detail, especially to the tender. The locomotive herself (yes, whatever their faults, engines are all feminine!) was renamed 'Hurricane' as a tribute to the aircraft which destroyed the most German aircraft in the 1940 Battle of Britain.

A pair of Hornby 0-6-0 tank engines, one in original Midland Railway finish, the other as LMS PN 7414, which I noted at Weeton, 4th May 1945, received added details. This *tour-de-force* for the RiMM, 'Traffic E' in GWR terms, was completed by two of that company's locomotives. An Airfix '2251' class mixed traffic engine was so good out of the box that I gave away an earlier model handbuilt by me! The second was 'Torquay Manor', a Mainline model, renamed as the first of the 78XX class, and reflecting a personal memory when, aged 12 in 1938, I saw her running in on a Gloucester-Ross-Hereford passenger train.

Because of my retirement from the London Borough of Southwark later in 1985, modelling ended in February. But, I had a go at converting a Triang clerestory to a first/Lav/third with Dean/Armstrong brake cylinders and modified bogies. The result was encouraging and I dug out from store a cast K's kit, of about 1967 vintage, for a 40ft passenger van. This was an interesting job, but the weight of the vehicle would make a train of similar construction too heavy just as, I gather from the model publications, the later generation of etched brass is proving. The grand finale at Keston was another K's kit for a six-wheeled 'Siphon' milk churn van and a Southern 'E 2' class 0-6-0 tank locomotive with extra weight and details. This locomotive was supplied directly to RiMM by HR Lines Esq, Director of Hornby – the circumstances of which I cannot now recall!

In July 1985 we moved to Ross-on-Wye, and the vast array of cardboard boxes in which RiMM was transported went into store. Such a hectic half of the year followed: wallpapering, and building kitchen cupboards, fitted wardrobes etc; but by the New Year 1986 the old bug bit again and I raked through the few remaining boxes which contained models requiring attention. I discovered that no real progress had been made for a museum building in Ross, but decided to carry on in order to be ready should this omission be remedied. I made a bench under the skylight upstairs and for the very first time in my sixty-one years - no longer had to clear up and put everything away at the end of each modelling session! The first job was to detail a Hornby North British 0-6-0 tank engine, to which I added the Old National No 4 Headcode for 'Express meat, fish, horse, cattle passenger stock' train. A Great Eastern luggage brake van was the first piece of rolling stock constructed at Ross: coach work by me, components below being Hornby six-wheel parts. I was fascinated by a refrigerator van, for the same company, originally built for the Italian butter traffic! I shortened a Hornby chassis and made the body myself. The very last entries in Black Book No 1 carry RiMM stock numbers R235 and 236 – in fact, marking the two hundred and thirty-sixth model in the collection. The models were modified Hornby LBSCR goods brake vans: one in pre-World War II livery, the other in wartime minimal lettering style.

Failure to raise adequate financial support led to building this small version by Fred Stone, at 55 Keston Road, Thornton Heath, Surrey. 'Open' for local occasions; showing Serena and Susan with the signs from the recently closed Ross Signal Box. 1969.

From 1967 until 1983, 'RiMM' also appeared at Fairfield Hall, Croydon, contributing a historic dimension to the Model Railways Shows. Miss Muriel Groves, who invented the title 'Railways in Miniature Museum' is seen with the Founder at Fairfield. 1983.

Erecting the baseboards and layout of 'RiMM' at Rowberry House.
The large water tank (centre, top picture) was a long-time land mark
behind Ross Station; one of three working level frames can be seen in the
foreground. Hundreds of metres of electrical wiring and steel wire-in-
tube, for mechanical operation of points and signal, involved months of
soldering – and agony under the baseboards! 1999.

It appears we settled in quite quickly at 'Chase Side' and between visits to Maude (Everall) and Jack & Celia Greep (Celia was Mary's twin sister), a string of models followed in 1986 including an unusually long six-wheeled van, at 34ft, for luggage and scenery on the London, Tilbury and Southend railway, plus no less than nine vans and wagons for the LMS! Three Midland vehicles included an implement truck with a South Midlands horse-drawn farm truck, a six-wheeled motor car van and a 'flat' conveying a 28ft rowing boat. A GW 'Macaw' conveyed a 'DUKW' amphibious carrier of the United States Army; an NE Bogie flat a 'Matilda' tank. On the agricultural front, and I consider it important for today's young people to have some idea of how hard was work on the land between the wars, a Southern 'Well E' carries a Binder and a GNR machine wagon conveys an East Anglian blue horse-drawn wagon. It is very relevant that RiMM should be representative of the railways at war in the twentieth century and I now quote from the Museum catalogue in this respect: The dark clouds of the First World War (1914–1918) were gathering and the enormous importance of mobilising the railways of Britain as the primary means of moving personnel, horses, materials, guns etc, was realized by 1912. In that year, the Railway Executive Committee was set up for the overall control of the lines with an element directly under the military and known as the Railway Operating Division, to function particularly abroad. The locomotives and rolling stock were branded: W ^ D (War Department). In September 1939 the Government resurrected the Railway Executive Committee although many preparations had been made in preceding years. Once again, rolling stock and engines directly under military control were so marked. Many veteran items served in both World Wars, often abroad on the European mainland, the Middle East, Turkey, Persia (Iran), Iraq etc. This section of the RiMM collection is a tiny representation of all this effort, and is offered as a tribute to the men and women whose war work, either as civilians or in the Forces, was **keeping the trains running**. It is no exaggeration to record that without the movement of traffic of every description in both World Wars by the home-mined coal-fired steam railways, Britain might well have been overrun and defeated.

One stalwart of both conflicts was the GWR Dean 0-6-0 mixed traffic tender locomotives of the 1890s! No less than a hundred and nine of these engines were requisitioned in World War II and a superheated version demonstrated, in 1950(!), superior steaming qualities to locomotives of later design. I modified a Mainline model and fitted a Westinghouse brake air compressor. As No 154 she is representative of a line of grand old warhorses.

The year 1987 began with a one-off: the L & SWR goods brake with a cattle drovers' compartment; also two other flat trucks for the same company, No 91, a road vehicle truck, carrying parts for a 'Big Willie' tank on an iron-wheeled trailer; and a United States horse-drawn army ambulance. An aeroplane truck conveys a disassembled British Sopwith Pup fighter aircraft – a reminder of the kite (RAF slang), which made the first successful landing on an aircraft carrier.

The existence of private owner vehicles on the railways proceeded as something of a love/hate relationship – largely because of reluctance of the non-railway owners to modernise the vehicles. However, such rolling stock is part of the railway picture of yesterday and today. In 1987 a private owner Moreland & Sons, 'England's Glory Matches' mineral open, by Mainline via Hong Kong(!) carries the 'return to' notice: 'When empty to Princess Royal Colliery Co Ltd, Whitecroft, Nr Lydney' – a lost Forest of Dean pit. Then an Esso oil tanker and a 20-ton open wagon lettered Cambrian Coke Co, the latter an example of the GWR's efforts to get private owners away from the 10-ton mentality; a Sheepbridge iron ore hopper of 1939; a Minerva Lime Company wagon and a rare Graham Farish van model, actually dated 20.7.79, being a Fyffes insulated banana van, for the conveyance of green bananas on way from the docks. Another Mainline, Hong Kong gem is a 3-plank stone wagon for E Turner & Sons, branded "Empty to Bizslade Siding, Severn & Wye Railway". A Mainline item, converted backwards from British Rail to GWR, with new buffers, is a 'non-common user' – 'Fruit A'. In theory, this branding meant that the LMS, LNER and SR should return empty such stock after unloading at their, the 'foreign', depots. Needless to say, whether the other rolling stock controllers obeyed this instruction depended upon how pressed they were at the time; getting **any** vans back in late November which could possibly be used for Christmas traffic was certainly a lost cause! A couple of GW 'Toads' (goods brake vans) followed: one vacuum brake fitted with screw-couplings, the other non-fitted and with the pear-shaped 'Instanter' coupling designed to absorb slack and nearly as effective as the screw type. An interesting six-wheeler was a gangwayed bow-ended brake van for the Great Northern, designed to match similar coaches of 1890.

A photograph of 1919, taken at East Croydon, showed an LB&SCR bogie flat wagon, loaded with two captured German guns. Considerable research, including the Imperial War Museum, was necessary to identify these artillery pieces. Indeed, I have just now (1996) unearthed the quarter-inch thick batch of photocopies from which, with the aid of Susan's massive German dictionary, I identified the guns and made drawings from the photographs. Eventually the models, incorporating many coloured pieces of plastic tube etc, were completed. Disappointingly, they looked like toys, **until** I applied the overall paint with the characteristic broken 'splodge' camouflage. The result is here for all to see; the sheer menace and deadly nature of the hardware cannot be denied and has been captured for posterity even though one-seventysixth full size! In the autumn of 1987, with the aid of *A History of GWR Goods Wagons*, I was able to bring to life a Wills Cigarette Card showing a Severn Tunnel goods brake van with metal gauge strips, looking like a hedgehog, and used to check clearances. Most boys of my generation had learnt about cars, warships, aircraft and railways from cigarette cards, which were usually accurately coloured. Only the better off among us could afford to fix them in the albums, although these were obtainable from the tobacconists for one penny each – equal to a half-penny in today's currency! The great multi-furrow Fowler steam ploughs always fascinated me – hauled back and forth across the fields by ploughing engines by the same Leeds maker. Several are still in use today. It is said that these great engines helped tow the Pluto petrol pipelines across the English Channel after 'D Day', 1944. The reversible plough model was made by me and sits in a well wagon of Mainline origin, liveried as a GWR 'Crocodile D' of 1909. John and Susan Gartside took me to Bovington Tank Museum, where we photographed and crawled around a 'Whippet' light tank of World War I. This I modelled, together with a suitable Midland Railway 'Warflat', and this brought a rather productive 1987 to a close.

The first models for 1988 slipped back in time to 1899 and the Highland Railway – an open carriage truck built at Inverness. The load is a horse-drawn hearse built in the same year and costing the considerable sum of £136 10s. A couple of tankers followed: Shell with lubricating oil, and a six-wheeler for British Vinegars. I got two cars in their right places next, **off** the road – a Bentley upon a GWR 'Scorpion' open carriage truck, as used for conveying cars under the River Severn, and a LNWR version of 1913, carrying a Sunbeam car of the same year. Then came a trio of LNER wagons: a 'Conflat S' with a road/rail container, a 'Lowfit' with a World War II General Stuart (Honey) tank and the longest British four-wheeled covered carriage truck (37ft 6in), code 'LLCK'. The latter I had noted full size at East Croydon Station in December 1966, carrying mail. The tiny *Model Railway News* monthly of November 1945 had carried drawings of a North British six-wheeled newspaper van which bore across the side, on a scroll about 12 feet long, advertising for *The Scotsman* published in Edinburgh. Quite fascinating this appeared. The heraldic design was described by Sir Eric Hutchison with full colour detail, 'Thistle-heads light magenta, white highlights and dark purple shading' – and so on. Quite a challenge to create and a joy to behold!

Something completely different is a Rhymney Railway Class 'R' mineral tank engine, built for working loose-coupled coal trains. An Ian Beattie drawing made this possible. I built the body in metal, using the old scratch building techniques I had used for the last forty-five years and with the same Solon 65 watt soldering iron! The final vehicle for 1988 was a LSWR Dining Car No 60, built in 1904, with electric lighting, gas cooking and a refrigerator. Drawings by G. R. Weddell and R. E. Tustin made a model practicable; coachwork of layers of thin card and tinplate underframe by me, upholstery and curtains by Sundour!

In 1989 I bought two kits by Parkside Dundas, a new maker of plastic mouldings of less familiar types of rolling stock. One was of a Southern four-wheel passenger brake van with distinctive two-way periscopes, enabling the guard to sight signals; the other, an SE & CR parcels van of 1920. A 1901 milk churn van body by Roxey, for the Somerset & Dorset, was mounted on an underframe by me. The agricultural scene featured in a couple of drop-side open wagons: Cheshire lines with a Croskill's clod crusher and a single-share horse plough; and a Great Central wagon with a Bickerton's sheaf delivery reaper completed with the aid of Batsford's *The Countryside between the Wars 1918–1940*.

A touch of exotica followed in the form of the Great Northern 'orchid van' of 1898, which conveyed these monocotyledons from Sander's Siding (St Albans) to King's Cross, London. What grand Victorian occasions were graced by these flowers? How interesting to contemplate where the delivery vans trotted around London's big houses and left these blooms! Anyhow, I built the van using Hornby components in the six-wheeled underframe. A handmade Great North of Scotland 3-plank open is curiously unique: it is the only wagon in the RiMM collection which has a drop-door on **one** side only – surely, a considerable inconvenience in practice! An LB & SC Machinery Truck of 1905 carries a neat two-wheel gig – an elegant little model to make with the aid of Lesney wheels.

The need to store the RiMM trains in storage sidings on view, but not actually running, gave me the idea to produce 'starting' signals appropriate to the company owning the trains. In fact, from August until December 1989, the files were examined and signals, with Peco solenoid motors, were turned out for the following companies: Midland, Great Eastern, Great Northern, LMS, Glasgow & South Western, GWR, SR, North Eastern, Highland, CLC, Midland & South Western Joint, LNER, and the Great Central. Some Ratio parts were incorporated, but most was handwork.

The year 1990 was also to be somewhat unusual on the modelling front although starting with rolling stock, namely the North Eastern Railway's elephant van. Like the Great Western, this was a one-off version of the DS 184 covered carriage truck, suitably strengthened. All handbuilt and with unusual spoked wheels for passenger rated stock. I then contemplated the layout of RiMM eventually and recalled that the only signal box so far completed was that at Ross on Wye. I looked through my building records and found quite a variety of old companies' boxes,or 'cabins' as some were known. One item I had in mind was a working set of level crossing gates so that a North British box which was located to work a crossing seemed appropriate – to get us away from the GWR! Drawings were available for the Ardlui box, situated between Fort William and Glasgow, and this is the basis for the model. Cardboard was used, reinforced with 5mm square wooden strips. The interior has the usual fittings including a 12-lever frame. For RiMM purposes the nameboard reads 'EMBIE

ROAD CROSSING' – giving a hint as to the company, but avoiding a recognisable setting, which the museum could not accommodate.

In the book *Modern Railway Signalling* c 1925 by Tweedie & Lascelles, I found a neat little box for the London, Brighton & South Coast Railway – a composite brick and wooden design, with 14 levers mounted on a massive 12in by 12in wooden beam! The gallery and ladder work is in metal, the body of card and wooden strips. Again, a non-prototype title for the nameboard was chosen and reads 'LONBRYTON'. In September 1990, I sought a contrasting design and found it in an LMS design of 1937, which clearly anticipated World War II. With reinforced concrete and 14in brickwork, these boxes were intended to give considerable protection against all but a direct hit by bombs. They had steel framed windows, toilet under landing and 25 levers facing rearwards. Many women were trained to work the boxes, in a little over three months! Distant points and signals required considerable strength even when the 'knack' was learnt. Fitted, as was LMS practice from 1935, with a nameboard at either end, I chose 'BLOCKHOUSE SIDINGS' as being quite appropriate! The rather grand finale for 1990 was a large overhead box as originally sited at Entwhistle, Lancashire & Yorkshire Railway. Such a design was expensive and quite exceptional, but sometimes restricted space made it necessary. The model girders are plastic with wooden columns and some metal work. The roof, upper interior floor and complete cabin are detachable from the girderwork. There are 29 levers, instrument shelf and all interior fittings. I have actually noted that there are 750 pieces in this cabin – which may explain why such elaborate models are seldom built! The fictitious name, which like the two others gives a simple clue to the originating company, although based on the practice of the Railway Signal Company Ltd, is 'LANYORK JUNCTION'.

At the turn of the year, 1991, I thought that something should be done about providing a rake of coaches for the Lancashire & Yorkshire 'Highflyer' Atlantic. Where coach kits were available they seemed now to be in etched brass and over £20 each. The weight would be a problem and I had been warned of the problems with trying to make long runs with soldered brass. Indeed, I had found something of the difficulties when making a GWR body about 1949! In particular, the heat can twist the body – for which like the Stirling aircraft at Melksham – there is no known cure! I sorted through books, photos and drawings and contrived a shortlist of five representative vehicles which could be formed as follows: open brake third, open first, first class kitchen car, open first/third and a first/third brake composite. Each has an underframe of metal (Castrol Oil can!), and a variety of bogies, 8ft, 6-wheel and Dublo conversions. The bodyworks are very individual, with fine white post card thick sides, reinforced with internal card, glazing and all the interior partitions and fittings – all on a one-sixteenth thick card base slotted out for four electric lighting bulbs in each coach. A statistical note on the brake composite: records show that it has 38 windows, requiring 456 cuts to clear the shapes. Also 120 punch holes one-sixteenth inch in diameter are required, the bottom drop-lights being straight line. No drawing was available for the kitchen car, but it was 'worked up' from the information in *LMS & LNER Historic Carriage Drawings*, *British Railway Carriages of the 20th Century Volume 1* and the No. 33 edition of the *British Railway Journal 1990*. The work occupied February to October 1991, and the five coaches look very interesting on the temporary track, which is all I have. So the 'Highflyer' will simply have to await a running-in working!

Thoughts travelled back to the four handsome corridor coaches for the North Eastern Railway, which I had finished in 1987. In *British Railway Carriages of the 20th Century Vol 1*, drawings and a photograph of a kitchen composite dining car for 1908, for the North Eastern, appears. This seemed an ideal centre vehicle for the set – 67ft long over body, on a massive and, I think, unique, bowstring underframe; mounted on six-wheeled bogies with gas cylinders and electric batteries, dual braked for both Westinghouse and vacuum. The cardboard body, fitted out with Sundour fabrics and on a Castrol can steel frame is a superb tribute to Edwardian coachbuilders, conveying both first and third class diners.

The most distinctive panelling etc of the Great Central Railway coaches made any conversions unlikely, but the open third excursion stock of 1910 was especially unusual. Known as 'Barnum's' after the style of the Barnum & Bailey's huge travelling circus of the time; with vertically planked teak sides, 60ft long and 9ft wide, these vehicles seated 64 passengers. The width was among the widest in use and the two open saloons would have given considerable impression of space and bulk – even elephant like! The model was completed by November 1991, on 10ft 6in wheelbase bogies. I 'laid' out half the saloon tables as for restaurant use.

That was to be the end of my railway modelling for several years as I switched, from the autumn of 1991 to October 1993, to constructing a one-eighth full size Second World War aircraft: the Mosquito Mark XV1 Bomber. Some 22 months to build a model, whereas the de Havilland home factory at Hatfield produced an average of **two** per **day** of the real aircraft for nearly four years!

Attention was then switched to researching for the 'Wilton Castle' Edwardian pleasure yacht, to be an exhibit for the Ross Heritage Museum. This proved to be a comparatively quick job, from August to November 1993, considering that no help other than three photographs could be found. Hence, I had to make the drawings and design the whole thing. It is electrically operated and radio controlled. Articles covering the construction are to be found in *Marine Modelling* for January and February 1995, and I am pleased to say that plans are available from Traplet Publications, Ref MAR 2433, Traplet House, Severn Drive, Upton-on-Severn, Worcestershire, WR8 0JL.

As they say, a change is as good as a cure(!) and November 1993 saw me looking back to the predecessors of the railways in Ross – in the form of the 1823 mail coach which rattled through the town to and from Milford Haven and London. Happily, drawings and some help with the wheel components and the horses was available for a 1in to the foot model. This occupied me until May 1994, and was a retrospective examination of the road coachbuilding technology, including such matters as the door drop-lights (opening windows) on leather straps, which was to come and survive for a hundred years or more in railway carriage design. As I write, early 1997, the coach awaits the opening of the Ross Heritage Centre, which has remained closed since 1988. Still, it is welcome to share my study at 'Chase Side'.

In September, 1994, I came back to the twentieth century with thoughts of the Railway Air Services. I had acquired two kits: a French Heller of the de Havilland 89A Dragon Rapide, and an Airfix Anson. The research involved recourse to my *Aeroplane Spotters* weekly journal of great importance in the war years to

Rex Nicholls and myself. The years 1945–6 were most helpful, showing that these aircraft worked the internal services in Britain including the Isles of Man and Wight. The Rapide carried eight passengers and the Anson seven! This was 1946 when the aircraft sported the silver livery with red and green lettering, carried for the short time before Railway Air Services became British European Airways. As with many of the real aircraft, I actually rebuilt the 'Annie' from its turret-fitted RAF role and it was quite a slow conversion. Still, both aircraft respresent a moment in time when flying **was** flying – not like the airborne Odeon cinemas of today! While in the Air Training Corps I had my first flight in a 'Rapide' from Croydon. It was said the driver was a fighter pilot 'resting'. He certainly side-slipped her down over the trolleybus wires and back to mother earth with expert ease. I did wonder, however, whether as many of the passengers were put off flying as received inspiration!

CHAPTER FIVE

Seventy Years-Old and Still Modelling: 1995

In the New Year, 1995, my eyes strayed upwards to the top of my wardrobe, where I still had a few boxes of unbuilt kits etc. Here, I unearthed a kit of the 'Noorduyn Norseman' by Matchbox. It was an aircraft of this type which took the American band leader, Glen Miller, to his death on 15th September 1944. I obtained R. C. Nesbit's book *Failed to Return* from the library and it seems almost certain that the Norseman, which had no navigator, might have been off course and in an area over the English Channel where the RAF would jettison spare bombs. It could have been flipped over if caught in this process. As I write, in September 1995, we see pictures of US aircraft returning from aborted raids to Bosnia and landing in Italy with 'FULL STORES' including 1,000 lb wing bombs. No-one did this intentionally(!) in World War II. The Norseman was a quite unique single-engined type, capable of carrying up to eight passengers. Only the pilot, Miller and Lt Col Baessell were on board on the fateful day. Using contemporary 1944 sources, I assembled the kit, with interior detail including a scatter of music scores with which Glen may well have been passing the time as the Pratt & Whitney radial roared away up front. So can a model hold a moment in time for posterity to **see**.

Pressures on my time otherwise took me away from the modelling bench for almost a year (will I **ever** retire?) and my attention in September 1995 turned to a P15 diagram GWR PN 14593 ballast wagon – rebuilt from a Triang drop-sided open of 1960 – numbered No 341 in the RiMM series. Another battered item, which I had picked up at a jumble sale about twenty years ago, was a French Jouef model, apparently based upon the GWR diagram P17 ballast wagon. Numbered 80158, this is finished as a non-runner to stand on the buffer stops at Ross – just as I photographed the full size wagon in 1964. As a non-runner, I chose to fit it with an 'instanter' coupling, to show how this with its pear-shaped middle link was designed to be levered down, by the shunter's pole, and so take up the slack between wagons.

This brought me to October 1995, and my 70th birthday. I looked back and thought that from the age of about eight years, I had used a safety razor blade, small saw, files and sandpaper to make all sorts of simple models. This continued through the war years and my life to date. Without fail, I could turn to the 'miniature' world for relief from present pressures and as a complete change from day-to-day life. This was particularly so when in September a non-melanoma, squamose spot erupted on my head and this was removed on 13th November 1995, at the County Hospital, Hereford. Unfortunately, this had to be repeated at the Wordsley Hospital, Stourbridge, where Mr Titley operated on 7th March 1996, repairing the deficit with a slice from my left leg!

In between all this excitement, in November 1995, I dug out a model I had made with little data in 1966 – a GWR bogie open wagon, telegram code 'Tourn'. This I had made from a Henry Greenly drawing in a pre-war book and a reference in the combined volume *History of GWR Wagons* by Atkins. This related how this vehicle, experimental in nature, was a 'one-off' and from 1888 to 1927 was rebuilt several times by Swindon shops. Most interesting was a later branding 'For use between Penarth Docks and Ely Paper Mill'. I engaged in a little detective/guesswork in this connection, discovering that esparto grass was imported from Spain and elsewhere – so this might have been the 'Tourns' load.

The New Year, 1996 found me cutting down a Dublo Open C tube wagon, fitting old type GWR oval coach buffers and new underframe detail. The result: a GWR sleeper wagon PN 14685, built during World War I, to diagram T 8. During recent holidays at Tenby I had acquired some Airfix WWII vehicles, and rail transport for them would have to be made. A GWR 'Macaw B' flat to J 28, bolsters removed, was an exercise in metal, with quadruple underframe and short self-contained buffers. Chained above is a K2 Austin ambulance and a K 6-wheeled RAF fire fighting crash tender. I added some details, including starting handles in place. In the RAF 'MT' everything was to hand for anyone to start up and drive! I was much taken by the illustration on page 68 of Peter Tatlow's *Pictorial Record of LNER Wagons*. This showed a single-plank wagon on which was mounted an RAF 'gas' bottle trailer. This was, indeed, the eight-cylinder oxygen wagon with the most unusual, apparently hydraulic, suspension. No drawing was available of the trailer, but I judged sizes from the wagon and my own experience; made drawings and constructed this most characteristic little vehicle. The rail wagon is a Bachmann, Chinese made (!), GWR match-truck, with a few amendments.

The White half-track from the USA, by Airfix, had a two-wheeled trailer and I dug out a long-saved Chinese-made jeep from a Christmas cracker! Suitably thinned out in detail, with steering wheel, gear lever, petrol tank, windscreen etc, this looks remarkably good. A 52ft bogie flat wagon, an LMS 40 ton 'BBZ', was made and long enough to accommodate these three items. This wagon, in metal and 208mm over headstocks, looks very impressive and so typical of those days around 'D Day' in June 1944.

The last little combination for March 1996 was an LMS bogie bolster 'B' of 40ft 9in over headstocks. This has a Playcraft frame over which a post card thick layer is added, rivets being impressed from the undersides. The load was the AEC Matador four-wheel drive artillery tug and the 5.5in field gun with muzzle and breech wrapped in canvas. All the heavy loads were fixed down with chains from old necklaces donated by Mary or the girls, each with a screw coupling wound and soldered up from a single length of wire. As I write this, Peter Churchas has just called to ask me to 'open' his model railway shop and exhibition in Cantilupe Road, Ross, on 29th March 1996. I must put the models aside and draft my speech! But, on the 19th March, I had to attend the Hereford County Hospital and Mr Butcher, of Gardner-Butcher garage, Ross, kindly took me in his car. We chatted and I asked whether he knew about the aeroplane his (?) grandfather had made in Ross in 1909. He answered in the affirmative, and said he would give me such photographs as he had and notes from the contemporary editions of *Flight*. This he did and I undertook to offer the completed aircraft to Ross Heritage Centre. Nothing more like a box-kite has come my way but its tiny engine and pilot, converted (drastically!) from a Chinese American girl rider, looks quite the Edwardian motorist/cyclist as he speeds across the ground.

Construction taught me much of the inherent weakness of such a main-frame, and one can only wonder at the extraordinary progress of flight which the 1914 war would so soon bring.

It was now early July 1996, and the railway shop 'opening' went well although I wore a home-made plastic disc over my left facial area to hide surgery; which was effected to remove a cancerous skin condition, probably related to my service in the RAF on the Gold Coast fifty years ago! In celebration of being alive, I went along to Peter's 'Totally Trains' and bought my first engine for perhaps twenty years! This is a Bachmann, Chinese made, LNER V2 No 3650 in black, early wartime lettering. Such engines took equal shares with the A4s on the 20-coach expresses London (King's Cross) to Edinburgh – which I had travelled on in 1947 when I escaped RAF Benson's 'bull' for Leuchars and Scots porridge! Only small touches of silver, white and copper paint were needed, plus lamps as 'Through Freight' headcode, new tender knuckle coupling and front locomotive screw-coupling. I seldom leave any type of 'model' coupling on the front of an engine where it is seldom used, but, so prominent if fitted. The fireman acquired an LNER (Roche drawing) shovel and the handles of pricker etc now protrude from the tender tunnel. The body was released by one bolt, under the rear pony truck, and the chassis and other bearings oiled with Castrol motor oil and Molyslip grease on the worm. The Chinese-made engine has split axles to facilitate current pick-up; this is even effected on the pony trucks. Tested on a single yard of Peco track, the Walschaerts gear lopes along with casual power. I long to see this engine on a wartime train giving young people a realistic idea of how steam transport was so crucial to our survival; and me and others of my generation a little of the nostalgia we probably deserve to enjoy!

At the end of 1996, I had considered the options for display of the eighth-scale model Mk XVl De Havilland 'Mosquito' bomber aircraft of Pathfinder Group, World War II. I decided to write to the Commanding Officer at Wyton, where a museum was being constructed in the Operations Room of the original Pathfinder base and planned to be open in 1997. I received an almost by return letter of acceptance, and on 23rd January 1997 Sergeant Peter Stanley, the museum curator and Corporal Paul Blakeborough, the station's best aero-modeller, arrived to take charge of 'U' Uncle. Both them and myself were glad I had spent much time making carrying cases for the wings and fuselage separately. These were well padded with sponge rubber for, as Paul the modeller said, moving models on the ground was the main source of damage! Daughters Serena and Susan videoed and photographed the scene and we were front page in the *Ross Gazette* on 6th February 1997. I was very pleased how well the four major bolts locked the wings to the fuselage, which went into place with a gentle puff of exhausted air from the joint; not bad a job since it was over three years ago she was built. She was equally quickly dismantled and loaded into a transit van, complete with all the books I had collected; also handbooks compiled during construction and which would aid any maintenance etc, in the future. I was a little sad as the family waved her off, but consoled by the promise we would meet again at Wyton on 27th July 1997 (coincidentally, my late mother's birthday) when the remaining Pathfinder Association folk would again gather. Overall, can the modeller's art be taken much further than to provide a commemorative item which will ensure all the sacrifices of Group 8 will not be forgotten?

The only engine in the collection which specifically awaited a train of coaches was the Great Central 'Atlantic' No 265 'Jersey Lily'. This was an area where brass etched kits occasionally became available. These were not only expensive, but also very heavy and there were doubts in my mind, as others also expressed, that this was not an ideal material, as I had found with a GWR first in 1948, which became permanently twisted when the plain brass was soldered. The usual searches through my LNER files revealed very little except some notes that the *Great Central* books, by George Dow, contained essential drawings and photographs. These comprised Vol 2 1864–1899, published in 1962 by Locomotive Publishing Company, and Vol 3 1900–1922, published in 1965 by Ian Allan. Fortunately, both volumes were obtained for £40, from Henry Wilson of Tarvin, Chester, CH3 8HB. Unfortunately, the drawings of the brake corridor composite (numbers 1684 and 1687) I made were to 3.5mm scale, as others in the book. Salvation was at hand through John my son-in-law's computer, which increased the dimensions by 16 per cent to just about 4mm scale. This machine also printed the sides using 130 gsm cartridge paper – almost thin card in nature – of which two layers comprised the bodywork. I had to cut and paste the compartment layout from the two compartment doors/window spacing shown on the corridor side. This gave me the two firsts and two thirds for the compartment side. This has worked quite well. Printing one side on pink paper and the other on white helped to keep construction clear. The curious handrails on these coaches are as though cut from signal ladders – so this is what I did from some 1960 brass pressings.

The first British buffet car, No. 1307, was similarly photocopied onto cartridge paper from the 4mm drawings by Eddie Davis in the *Railway Modeller* of June 1981, supplemented by an interior view on page 277, *GCR Vol 2* by George Dow. A quite fascinating vehicle, particularly with the buffet etc, inside. The entire set, including the earlier built 'Barnum', has four 3 volt bulbs wired in series in each vehicle. Note that the roofs are glued in place so it is necessary to cut holes in the floors so that the bulbs on leads are inserted like street lamps. The electrical joints are soldered between the solebars on the underside of the floors – so that removal of the bulbs on the wire stems is relatively simple. At the loco end of each coach are contacts shaped from 5mm wide phosphor bronze strip, drilled and bent to admit a 14mm pin which carries a loop of wire from the vehicle in front.

Coach No. 1299 is a corridor lavatory composite with luggage compartment, as shown in photographs *GCR Vol 2* page 273. Drawings can be found in *British Railway Carriages 1901–1922* by David Jenkinson, on page 168. This coach and the buffet are finished in the early French grey and brown livery whereas the brake composites are in the 1904 livery of cream and brown. This latter finish is well depicted on page 145, *GCR Vol 3*, although the vehicle there illustrated is a luggage, not brake, composite No. 1703.

The computer, this time my own, was most helpful in printing out on type faces 4 and 5, the large amount of lettering on the GCR stock. This probably explains why they are rarely modelled and why the doyen of GCR modelling, the Rev Peter Denny, admitted that only a 'suggestion' of the lettering was possible in 4mm scale. However, the new technology, printed on the thinnest available paper fixed with clear wallpaper pastes, provides black shaded lettering to which a touch of gold can be added to the left.

No doubt the Chinese will do it better in due course!

These four coaches occupied January to August 1997,

working most afternoons.

I cannot allow the summer of 1997 to pass by without recording a visit Susan made possible for Serena, Mary, little Michelle and me to RAF Wyton Pathfinder Museum, to see how my Mosquito 'U' Uncle had settled in. Fate had arranged this special occasion on 27th July, which was my mother's 110th birthday in spirit. It was indeed a proud moment to be photographed with the model, and a bonus when Sgt Peter Stanley, the curator, told me that the 1944 navigator had examined the aircraft and exclaimed, "That's **my** kite!" – with considerable amazement! Could there be any greater satisfaction for a spare-time modeller of special memories...?

From May 1997, Michael Aslanian and myself struggled to reach an acceptable agreement for the permanent showing of the models, mail coach, steam yacht, butcher aircraft and the RiMM models. This was eventually reached on 26th September 1997, and will run for a year when, subject to any variations we agree, continue. Barbara Jordan, solicitor, drew up the Agreement and also sought charitable status for RiMM from the Commission. This is an exceedingly drawn-out process and we have to be sure that the collection **cannot** under any circumstances fall into the Commission's hands. Hence, we have rejected Clause S in the Agreement. It is my heritage to my family, **not** to a shower of bureaucrats who have done nothing to deserve anything.

Much more productive, since the autumn, has been the tidying up of the RiMM boxes in the loft. I began to get increasingly concerned about the delay in completing the showcases for the large models, but realised I must prepare the old trackwork, repair buildings, overhaul the signals etc, so that all may be rapidly put in place. This work went well and brought back memories of Keston Road, my *Model Railway Constructor* articles of over thirty years ago and, of course, the real Ross Station, 'Rybro' etc, etc.

As I sorted out the items, I decided to examine each engine as it appeared. By mid-December I had checked over 30; only the North Eastern compound remains hidden deeply in some box. Most alarming has been to discover its brother 'Atlantics' (Great Central, and Lancashire & Yorkshire) have 'lost' their power sources! This is due to brittle fracture of the old Trix motor frames – for which there is no cure and no direct replacement. The solution, I fear, is to try and unbuild the tenders to take the modern motor units of the Hornby short-wheelbase tender power units. Happily, I chose David Gibbs of Cambridge to renovate some other units and am in the process of obtaining a Dapol 14XX chassis/motor for our '4855', whose gear wheel has become completely toothless! As it was the authorised supplier of spares locally, I telephoned Hereford Model Centre, Commercial Road, on 12th December 1997, and the owner said he would search for the X 942 tender units I needed for the 'Atlantics'.

Meanwhile, the Dapol 0-4-2 chassis for '4855' had arrived, but proved devilish difficult to 'retrofit' into my metal bodywork – wartime dried milk tins material! Most of December was occupied in slimming down the magnet block of the motor and it is now a simple push-fit to the body; coupled to the trailer (auto-coach). It was a great pleasure to see the unit smoothly functioning once more. As far as I can recall, this became the fourth power/ chassis for this locomotive and just goes to show that I was right in my original conviction that RiMM models, however to scale and handbuilt the bodywork, would need to accept commercial underpinnings which could be regularly replaced.

Progress on the baseboards for the railway models in the Antique Centre gallery was exceedingly slow, but the two 4ft 6in supersize train turntables were completed by Matthew of Kemps on 25th April 1998. This gave me an insight into the track on the table and how this would be likely limited to two display tracks either side of the central axis... This could give quite some space within the circuit, at either end turntables, on which virtually independent displays could fit and be changed from time to time. My mind turned to the two Railway Air Services aircraft I had available and the possibility of a suitable setting for a small airport. This would need a control tower and I turned up my photograph of the Little Staughton tower I had seen in 1992.

This seemed quite a useful basis as I could trace no RAS photographs from my considerable records. During January 1998 a model emerged with concrete finish and flat roof; quite atmospheric and to the tiny scale that was flying in the immediate post-war period. The detachable roof would enable lighting to be fitted if this becomes practicable on the giant turntable. Poring over the drawings for Ross Station, I explored once more the problem of getting the auto-train to leave the Bay platform and quite quickly disappear towards Monmouth.

The idea of a tunnel came to mind and I began upon an 18in base which would be adequate to hide the little train. This has cardboard 'ribs', rather aircraft-like in structure, covered with strips of paper and very old towelling. Some experimental green spray shades were obtained from a car shop and it was found that with Lada Green, touched up with Humbrol yellow undercoat, the most natural finish was obtained. A box of 'Merit' miniatures produced two families of sheep and lambs, which are arranged climbing up the paths across the tunnel. This proved fascinating to my four-year-old granddaughter, Natalie, so I have pleased somebody! At the Ross end is the simple portal at Symonds Yat, whereas the further end is in Bath stone – a single-track version of that found between Bath and Bristol at Twerton-on-Avon, typical of those some landowners insisted upon when the lines were built to blend in with their estate buildings.

Mary's gift to me of a Hornby engine turntable needed some attention as it is not designed for access to the motor and gears without lifting it from the layout. The mechanism cover is now released by two side-mounted self-tapping screws, so simplifying access for maintenance *in situ*. The cabin was changed to brick paper finish, glazed etc, with general dirtying up of the ground base. *The World's Railways and How They Work*, published by Odhams in 1947, proved to be helpful in illustrations from LMS layout of motive power; this guided fitting the vacuum apparatus whereby the engines turned themselves by vacuum ejector power.

The short days of February 1998 rushed by and the Ross layout drawing brought attention to the need for at least half a dozen GWR buffer stops. Luckily, the photographs taken in the early 1960s included them, and other files contained a selection of M. S. Cross's drawings and photographs. This enabled me to bend and solder some old 4mm scale rail into 'stops' – following the practice of the full size companies! Despite a wish to give as wide of variety as possible elsewhere on the layout, the details cover only GWR, Great Central, SE & CR, L & SWR, Midland, and the Great Eastern. Such a necessary item had such a long life normally, but hardly engendered much interest until they stopped a runaway engine or piece of rolling stock!

The saga of getting Hornby short-wheelbase tender units 'X 942' from the Hereford spares dealer got further and further into chaos as the wrong units – a four-wheel diesel version – arrived! I had three, and after checking the tiny wheelbase of the L & Y 'Highflyer' engine's tender, decided I would have to take the only course available and build the 4-wheel unit into a piece of rolling stock as might be permanently coupled to tender. I chose an L & Y horse box arranged to take current from the tender, light the engine's firebox and link into the coaches' lighting system. This was not as difficult as seemed at first likely and it was a real pleasure to see loco, tender and horse box (latter moderately weighted with lead) move gently around with surprising over-run from the ring-field spur gear motor driving two rubber tyred wheel sets. Then I received a phone call from Hornby saying they had "discovered" that what I really needed with 6ft 6in spaced axles, was what they used in the 'Patriot' locomotive tenders. The only snag was that the next factory 'run' would not be until **July 1998** – but I am assured that the units would be forwarded via the Hereford dealer. Well, after six months' delay – there seems no alternative but to hope for the best!

Having thought about displays for the space either side of the track(s) on the big turntables, I felt that the engine turntable could be accommodated on one segment together with the LNER wagon tippler coaling plant and could stand accompanied by the usual accoutrements of a depot: ash pits, sand, water hydrants etc. However, the essential component of a locomotive servicing was missing, namely, an engine shed much more modern than the broad gauge conversion at Ross! Checking the files, and Edward Beal's books, I concluded that a modernised Midland Railway design seemed to offer an interesting model. April 1998 found a two-road brick built shed under construction with isolated track so that up to four locomotives could be stabled under control.

During April 1998, Jeremy Whitehouse, a local artist, called at Chase Side seeking help regarding railway backgrounds for his pictures. I showed him the collection of negatives and suggested Jack Coombes might be willing to help him with prints selected from my catalogue. He showed me some magnificient paintings of Spitfires, Hurricanes, Walruses etc, and I was able to show him my *Aeroplane Spotter* pictures of an Avro York, which is his likely next commission. A recent addition of *Model Collector* revealed that Corgi have produced two York models, and Jeremy is likely to acquire one to suspend and paint in flying attitude. This is a novel idea to me, but just goes to show how uniquely good models of any non-available full size object are so valuable. Jack later told me he had been able to help with railway prints.

The inspection pits were incorporated in a baseboard for this shed with the track coming in upon quarter-inch foam ballast strip. The pits were lined with engineers' blue brick paper and, although a little shallow, are the best practicable to prepare at home and without cutting the train turntable base upon which it would stand. There are the usual offices: for foreman, stores, mess room; and, in the main building: lathe, large plane and forge. Two internal lights are fitted and I think, with Slater's workers in intelligent poses, quite an imposing piece has resulted. By deliberate design, the walls and roof merely fit over the base containing the rails. Consequently, lifting the 'building' clear will give access to the track throughout. Son-in-law, Haydn, asked whether the windows were bought in. "No," says I, "handwork with bow pen and brush." I think he approved and despite his professional expertise in full size painting was glad I had done it myself!

I have been conscious throughout the years that although the Southern Railway operated minimal freight services compared with the other Big Four operators, there was little information in my hands as to post-1923 built goods stock. One such I traced backwards from British Rail *Classification of Special Wagons* giving the painted numbers of 32 'Lowmacs' (machinery well wagons) built under SR Diagram 1681 about 1938 – this in anticipation of WW II by all the British companies. I modified a Hornby model with a Matchbox Allchin tractor as load.

I had acquired an Airfix model of a private owner (John Arnold & Sons of Chipping Sodbury, Glos) quarry operator and now loaded with 'stone': actually, dried tea bag contents glued to a card/newspaper base. Nice change from PO coal wagons, which however vast in numbers full size, would be quite overwhelming in RiMM if so proportioned. My beady eye, in May 1998, also fell upon an unboxed kit of black parts in store. This was for a nine-compartment non-corridor bogie coach, completely void of any manufacturer's name. Careful search through my records eventually revealed a close resemblance to the rebuilds of four- and six-wheeled stock which the Southern made in the 1920s and 30s, on new underframes, for suburban use. A photograph, page 24 of *BR Carriages of the 20th Century, Volume 2,* by David Jenkinson, gave me the idea and brought back personal memories of Thornton Heath–Victoria years as a commuter. Nine – or ten-compartments would have as many as twenty(!) **standing** on the feet of the ten sitting in awful times of dense fog, cancellations etc, when passengers just fought to get in and get **home!** Almost 300 persons per coach and the springs down to the 'stops' as we bounced over the awful Southern track. Then I came upon an advertisement of 1969 for a Graham Farish kit, based on BR practice but encouraging additions to follow earlier company practice. Indeed, I had fitted LSWR ventilators and the 13s 9d kit came to life in post-war minimal livery.

Packed in its own tiny cardboard box I found a Wills rail cleaning wagon based upon an actual SECR open – fitted with sprung brushes to keep grease off the rails down to Folkestone Harbour. This is designed to take cigarette filters, two mounted vertically, above each running rail. I will certainly try this out on the RiMM layout because even in Ross there is considerable grime to be kept at bay; the Achilles heel of all miniature displays. Last of this Southern batch of May 1998 models was an ABS kit for an iron gunpowder van, similar to those used on the LNWR and GWR. This one is ex-LSWR, finished in Southern Railway 1930s style. Probably quite surprising to modern eyes is the fact that the gunpowder contents were so advertised – although sometimes abbreviated as 'GPV' – little powers of deduction were involved. Just shows how well behaved was the population in earlier days.

Three Ratio kits for GWR items came to hand from the old stock box. The first was for an 'Open C' with 24ft 6in loading space and built in 1914. It would carry the long loads of both World Wars and became more usually known as 'Tubes' later on. The load for PN 67878 is a simple boat trailer, lifted in over the sides and roped down through the steel rings on the top planks. The remaining plastic kits are Ratio four-wheel GWR five-compartment non-corridor coaches from the 1880–1900 period. These required compartment divisions, seats, upholstered in as near as I could get to 'rep' from the Sundour 'Express' range of pre-war fabrics. Metal wheels, with MJT Mansell inserts, top-hat brass bearings, and simple metal-plank-with-hole for my vacuum pipe and screw coupling, complete the hardware.

Some Slater's passengers were installed and the long process, some ten days, was occupied in applying the ornate livery. Each has the GWR insignia: the intertwined pre-1910 GWR and the other with the arms within a garter in 1900 style. The vacuum cylinders were arranged in the Dean/Armstrong fashion and wire 'pipes' link the gas lights on the roof to the supply carried up one end from the tank below. Perhaps most trying (or tiring!) for this 72-year-old was the 'THIRD' class lettering on each of the twenty doors on the pair. Sigh of relief when the coat of gloss varnish was eventually applied!

Next discovery was three Model Wagon Co, Seamill, Ayrshire, kits for cattle wagons from 'over the border', namely: North British, Highland and Glasgow & South Western, plus a 6-ton van for the latter company. These kits were in sharp contrast to the Ratio plastic and of white metal throughout including even the buffers, which, in my view, are much stronger executed in brass although some loss of bolt head detail comes with turned items. I replaced the thin plastic sheet, supplied for roof and floor, with cut-up AA and bank plastic cards for the latter. Posterity may, in due course, discover my signature trampled by miniature cattle in these trucks!

The flimsy bend-on-the-grooves in the brass-compensated Mallard units was reinforced with Evostick in the grooves. Metal wheels in top-hat pointed bearings proved satisfactory. I test by Evosticking the bases approximately lined up with the spring centres – then rolling each wagon down a tilted tray. This will indicate if the axles are not at right-angles, and a quick push with a miniature screwdriver will get alignment right. Note that this is better than using a length of track, which will itself guide a defective setting, until it reaches a point when any deviation will demonstrate itself. The detail of these white metal kits is undoubtedly good, but the weight and some flimsiness in the buffers is disadvantageous. I used copper computer wire for the iron bars on the sides as it makes a stronger job than the plastic rod supplied.

Mid-June 1998 found me searching through the pending boxes and extracting what I believe is the last trio of ready-to-run models. They are an Airfix 1975 GWR Conflat with furniture container, a Hornby Consett iron ore hopper with opening bottom doors, and a Lima of Italy six-wheel Co-operative Wholesale milk tanker. A more Catholic collection it would be difficult to find! All needed my standard knuckle coupling, fitted with some difficulty; including the need to tap and thread the heavy cast buffer beam of the hopper to take a bolt. Research revealed suitable numbers and, with a vacuum cylinder added, the Conflat became PN 39325 of Diagram H7. Less emerged on the tanker, but some notes I had made fifty years(!) ago in the GWR Rolling Stock Department, Paddington, indicated the likely painted number as '2520' from a 1933 batch. A blank was drawn for the provenance of the hopper, although many similar wagons were being built in the 1940s for the LNER. A single drop of Castrol motor oil in each axle bearing completed the work and the trio glided away down the test track – no doubt glad to be free of their boxes!

While awaiting the baseboard construction at the Antiques Centre, I moved to prepare strips of foam for under track ballast. I had tried this idea many years ago at the Keston Road layout, where sawdust, tea leaves etc had also been considered. My natural instinct (frustrated engineer!) was against the granite dust which some modellers were using. However stuck fast, I always feel this to be an area of dubious permanence because of the danger of gluey/oily dust in mechanisms, bearings and pointwork. The fact that a plastic foam means one is technically viewing 'holes' instead of 'stones' is something I can live with from normal viewing distance of two or three feet. Further away it does not matter and best of all is the slight springiness of the foam – quite like the movement observed in the full size trackwork – and the sleepers will bed in naturally.

This resilience seems to give the locomotives the edge upon starting trains – in effect, the engines and rolling stock are upon a sprung surface, which obviates the need for tricky springs in 4mm scale on individual vehicles! Close to a perfect solution and needing minimal fixing down except at point lever locations. I had long hoarded any foam plastic in the region of a quarter-inch in thickness, and much of the first six months of 1998 was taken up cutting this into 45mm strips for single track, and 85mm for double track. In this matter the underscale Peco 27mm and Hornby 29mm sleepers contribute to our illusion of getting more than strictly possible into the limitations of an indoor model railway. The foam takes water-based paints, such as Dulux vinyl matt, mixed on the spot to your desired colours at many ironmongers. I chose a Khaki shade for overall finish – darkened in some places, lighter in others.

Best of all is that the drumming sound of models on hard ballast is absorbed by the foam and the stock seems to glide along the rails. My collection of foam ranges in depth from 2mm, which will be ideal for Ross goods yard; the rest, nominally one quarter-inch deep, varies from about 5 to 6.5mm. Originally, I had intended the baseboard surface to be tipped slightly forward, so that the trains at the rear would be more easily seen. However, this would present ballast problems to keep the sleepers and rolling stock upright needing to be shallow at the front, higher at the rear edge with some potential problems at points. I aim to try and employ the different foam heights in order to inject variation in the sighting, the deepest level being at the rear of the baseboard.

It may be useful to record the source of some newly acquired foam, which was discovered by daughter Serena. I bought twenty-five strips 48in by 45mm wide (100ft run) from Knit & Sew, 21 Winchcombe Street, Cheltenham, Glos, for £6 including postage, in July, 1998. It was cut into 45mm strips by the owner, who can supply any width or length required. Unfortunately, it is necessary to 'shoulder' the ballast by scissors and handwork! About every four strips it is necessary to oilstone the blades as the foam is an incredibly blunting agent. I am looking forward to setting this stuff in place, and hoping I've prepared sufficient mileage!

Into August 1998, excitement centred upon a box from Hornby containing three tender motorised units, Ref X 2034, allegedly for 'Lord Rathmore' locomotives, so a helpful 'Brian' explained to me from Margate. Never having heard of an engine of this name, the author was pleasantly surprised to find the wheelbase to be approximately correct for my 'Jersey Lily' tender – particularly allowing for the larger wheels than I had originally fitted. The unit was complete with axleboxes and springs, not unlike those needed; and even painted a plum shade very close to GCR livery! The most shattering thing was how to get this unit into a completely finished tender, with golden coats-of-arms, lettering and lining. Inspiration came eventually: it would be necessary to make a horizontal saw-cut all around the tank at running-plate level, in order that the body may 'sit' upon the new unit. Using the remarkable X-ACTO USA fine tooth saw, it was possible to handhold padding around the body, on its side, and gently cut through the soldered joint.

Completing this without damage to the livery was a great blessing and the wiring in commenced. This involved arranging the common-side (non-insulated wheels side) of the engine to convey current by a coupling plate which was drilled to plug into the tender's vertical pin. The other side was picked up by the non-tyred side of the tender. A little complication was to carry that current, via one of my painting brush ferrules bucket-type connectors, back to the engine's firebox bulb. The usual 14mm pin connections escape in insulated wire, through two notches in the tender body underside, to the coach sockets. A little bending of my 'coal' base fitted over the motor bulge and was spot-glued into position.

The important point is that the old metal tender body just 'sits' on the Hornby plastic running-plate so is easily removed for servicing the motor. I oiled up the 'Jersey Lily's' bearings and attached the new tender power unit. What a relief to watch the wonderful illusion of the Atlantic pulling away, the marine big-end rising and falling – new life indeed for the old warhorse! I still haven't located the North Eastern Atlantic buried (with its train!) somewhere in the attic, but if it needs the same treatment, the X 2034 would seem suitable.

My hands turned to the 'unmade' box again and unearthed a Keilkraft of Lancing, kit No K309, of a Thorneycroft one-and-a-half-ton GWR parcel van. I cannot date the kit, but perhaps c 1970. A large coloured picture on the box shouts 'crude', but on the kit the main fault seems the completely smooth tyres. Whether this was correct or not when I was born (1925) I don't know, but each wheel was chucked in the vice and three longitudinal cuts made with the X-ACTO saw, then lighter cross-wise, making a more realistic finish. Tiny pin gear lever and soldered up handbrake improve the open driving area so reminiscent of the horse-drawn vans which were still operating during the 1920s–1940s period.

Among my valued books is a blue paperback *Measham Register of Motor Index Letters and Numbers* (with register of Authorities) 4th Edition, 7s 6d, published 1954–5. From this was selected a Wiltshire registration for the van as probably appropriate – 'MR' issued 1924 to 1947. My elder daughter kindly made the number plates by printing them very tiny on the computer... such is the joy of combining ancient and modern! Two coloured posters: Great Western Railway Pack No 73, from Tiny Signs 1998, are added to the kit's transfers. The whole was finished off with Humbrol matt varnish. Looking across the room to the vehicle, about four feet away, the result is most attractive. The author would like to find a modern, well post-World War II Thorneycroft as I photographed in 1960. It was at Ross and registered JXA 682 – a London registration 1947–50 flatbed bodywork.

Three more road items came to hand in August 1998: a Budgie crane wagon No 22, which needed glazing with plastic scraps, as also a Volkswagen car, Hong Kong built, saved from a Christmas cracker – nothing wasted here! A very battered Lesney Guy Otter pantechnicon appeared with layers of paint below which the word 'Pickfords' was just discernible. This was repainted medium green with yellow lettering, helped by an old *Radio Times* advertisement supplement of March 1974, which shows, in colour, Pickford vehicles through the ages. It is only about 3mm scale so will stand towards the rear of the display.

A non-road item, also by Lesney, appeared – a caterpillar tractor by the company of that name, Caterpillar Tractor Co, Peoria, USA. This involved a visit to the library and finding (in the children's section) a book *Change on the Land* by Gibbard, Farming Press. This revealed that the 'D8' cast on the model was probably built 1946–7 so just squeezes into the RiMM period. A new 'hollow' exhaust pipe was fitted, as was a tarpaulin over the seat. An Airfix, Hong Kong, Lowmac EU became LNER Lowmac EP paint number 260862. Chaining down the caterpillar and fitting a small vacuum cylinder at each end finished an attractive peacetime picture.

On 10th September 1998 Fred Hall telephoned to say that the

baseboards were complete at the 'Railway Gallery' in Ross Antiques Centre. Almost a year has passed since the project started and it was with some relief I panted up the steps and gazed at the vast (58in) turntables, set each end of the three 6ft straight sections. I paid up Fred's invoice of £325 and congratulated him upon a solid job. The next stage seemed to be to fit instrument boards, about seven inches below the bases, 7in wide and the full length of each section. This would give a 6ft run on each with ample room for controllers, switches and lever frame. The arrangement would easily accommodate the frames I have collected over the years; fifteen levers to the left of Ross, twenty-eight for the station area and about sixteen for the right hand section, which are yet to be purchased. In effect, the outstationed frames would be handling the non-Ross operational area, with some points and the collection of non-GWR signals.

These amounted to sixteen single arm examples including LSW, LNW, L & Y, Caledonian, LMS, Midland, Great Eastern, Great Northern, SR, North Eastern, Highland, CLC, M & SWJ, LNER, and Great Central. In addition, five 'splitting' junction bracket signals, which seemed, providentially, adequately to meet the needs of the new layout. I oiled up the multitude of pivots and removed some Triang point motors earlier fitted. Hopefully, the steel wire through copper tube method would be more appropriate to RiMM than electrical operation although doubtfully more cheaply since £82 of tubing is involved!

Fred had a scheme for a length of piano hinge supporting a six-foot-long drop flap across each control board. He also would make and fit sliding doors below to make useful storage space, and finish the carpentry. It took another month for him to be available to finish the work, for £374, and 10th September 1998 found us contemplating what was left to be done. I had found suitable locks, from Arnold & Ridley's shop, for the sliding doors and Michael Aslanian said he would contact his varnishing man to match the finished cabinets to blend with the gallery rails. Crawling underneath, I again remarked upon the need for electrical socket outlets – one double socket in the centre of the straight sections. Michael suggested I contact Anthony Haile, the local electrician who had previously worked on the premises.

We have reached the stage whereby I needed to contact the 'plastic' people at Newport about overall coverings to protect the layout from dust, overactive fingers etc. The firm put me in touch with a technical subsidiary at Cleobury Mortimer and, at 14th September 1998, I await this development with some anxiety. I have provided the drawings requested but I suspect this will be a distinctly 'one-off' job. There is a cast acrylic 3mm clear plastic available, said to be ten times stronger than glass, which I have mentioned to this firm. No doubt, some sort of aluminium framing may also be necessary. Standing in the gallery, I am concerned that both myself(!) and visitors should enjoy the window seat. Fred suggests this be made in three sections by Downings of Ross. Again I produce drawings and take them along for discussion. The owner said he has heard of some new reasonably priced uncut moquette which would be ideal. He will see me with samples shortly.

So here we are, mid-September with Michael hoping for an autumn opening of the Railway Gallery, but me saying that "Christmas, 1998" is much more likely in view of the quite enormous amount of work necessary after the real tradesmen have departed!

The writer seized the, hopefully short, period left, while Mr P. Gardiner is called in by Michael Aslanian to varnish the baseboard cabinets in the same shade of dark mahogany as will match the general Antiques Centre furnishings. Having the baseboard control shelves in place drew my mind to consider the lever frames and their fitting. It was decided to put the frames onto centimetre thick sub-boards, 3in wide, which could accommodate a length of 2mm copper wire, bent at right-angles at each end and set into the boards. Set about an inch from the back of the lever frames, this would be the 'anchor' point to which the end of the copper tubes could be soldered. A couple of holes were drilled in each board so they could eventually be screwed to the shelves, but meanwhile there would be merit in leaving the frames and base loose for easy access with the soldering iron.

Another matter occurred to be solved: that of cutting the dozens of track lengths to fit across what appears to be a vast space of baseboarding! The author resolved this to some degree by making a 'rail clamp' device – namely two lengths of 18in board,

Jersey Lily nick-named Great Central Railway Atlantic 4-4-2 express Passenger locomotive by J. G. Robinson. The corridor train includes PN 1307, the first British Buffet Car of 1899.

View over the Hereford end of Ross station showing the goods shed and a variety of loaded wagons conveying farm machinery, timber, coal from local collieries and gas wagon for carriages.

Monmouth Bay with 48xx Class 0-4-2 tank engine No. 4855
with push-pull Trailer coach on Ross – Monmouth route.
Boy in foreground is Founder of *Railways in Miniature* in 1938.

Looking towards Gloucester from Ross includes Glasgow & South Western
PN 102 Class 45 0-6-2 Tank engine with a World War I freight;
red crosses mark a World War II LNER ambulance train.

LMSR Beyer Garatt PN 4975 2-6-0 + 0-6-2 freight locomotive
as built in 1930; known for 1000 tons coal trains to London.
Demonstrated in unpainted condition for modellers.

The LNER Coaling Plant was electronically operated and built by
Mitchell Converyer Co., London. The two-road Engine shed is
based upon Midland/LMSR practice as renovated in 1930s.

Great Eastern 'Norfolk Coast Express' behind PN 10 Class P 43 Single-wheeler 4-2-2 locomotive. Railway Air Services and display board relating to renewing Wye Valley Railway.

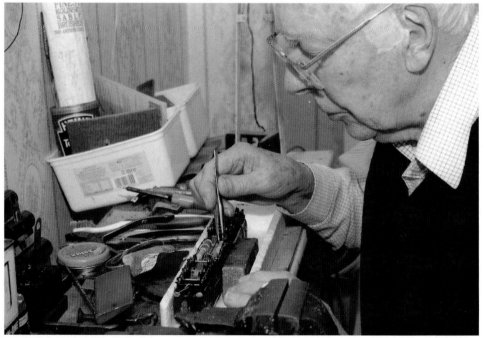

Diamond Jubilee partnership: The Author and the American vice shown both flew home from Accra, Gold Coast (now Ghana) by Lancaster in 1947. He is now, in 2007, 82 years of age.

The handsome Great Eastern single, of James Holden's design in 1898, may be compared with William Dean's version shown elsewhere. PN 10 has working parts between cylinders and axle.

Based on Entwhistle, Lancashire & Yorkshire Railway, this overhead signal box is as of the Railway Signal Company Ltd. Three special vans NE refrigerated, Butter and Banana visable.

Great Central Express Atlantic locomotive PN 265 shown as built by
Beyer Peacock in 1904 livery; it is leaving Ross after overhaul;
hand-built five coach corridor train.

Ross-on-Wye from Hereford end; showing North Stafford Class K 4-4-2
tank engine on test and passing LNER bogie flat TC conveying
a World War II first lease-lend United States fighter.

Author is painting a Midland coach after the initial coat of shellac has dried. 'River Fal' with the three coach corridor set for the Gloucester–Ross–Hereford line.

Approaching Ross from the West with three-arm GWR signal covering the platform road and freight lines either side. The Great Central PN 265 express engine and train to left.

GWR Bulldog No. 3431 River Fal 4-4-0 tender engine on test bench with the usual three coach corridor train on Hereford–Ross–Gloucester service. MR clerestory roof coach awaiting painting.

A close-up of the Midland and Furness engines both of which appear to be in-steam. Actually, the 'smoke' has been donated by the domestic cat; it is glued to lead shot!

two and three-quarter inches wide and three-quarters of an inch in thickness. They are joined down one side by two hinges and in the sandwich formed are stuck two strips cut from an old table mat, spaced to just accept the sleeper ends of Peco track. This device, padded between the rails with loose card strips, will hold the track firmly down by one hand; the other cutting with a fine tooth saw. The method of dealing with track curved to suit the layout would be to mark, with the excellent W. H. Smith label pen, the rail breaks needed, tapping the sleepers back into a straight line before inserting the length in the rail clamp. The pen marks are then nicked with a rat tail file to guide the saw. Hopefully, a useful device.

Looking at the 6 volt rechargeable battery, now removed from the 'Wilton Castle' yacht, the writer decided to build it on to an angled wooden train which would hold the battery upright. This, with a little weighted wooden block on a lead, with brass drawing pins inserted underneath, would act as a portable testing unit upon newly laid track. A similar block simply fed a 12 volt bulb in a small wooden box through which it glowed through a porthole and is protected from being easily damaged. Hopefully, this simple combination will help speed up laying the trackwork, testing the 16-switch panel of ex-World War II aircraft switches which control 'dead' sections etc, without having to get a remote controller functioning all the time.

Drawing out the track layout, showing **both** rails for the first time, drew attention to the problem of controllers and how to wire them. Although the track layout is closely dependent upon the narrow gallery space, the primary matter is to accommodate Ross Station as the essential heart of the project. In effect, the 'main lines', double-track, from Hereford and from Gloucester, form the centre section of the display and will need a separate controller. One should be sufficient as only a single train would be operating at a time: for example, train from Gloucester arrives; train from Hereford runs in and stops; they leave separately. In the writer's mind, he sees controller 'B' in charge of these lines.

In front of these lines, to the viewer via a single-slip, are the goods shed and yard, and also at the Gloucester end, the Monmouth bay passenger platform, the 'Brunel' engine shed and the tunnel hiding the line disappearing down the Valley. This section seems to need another controller, which RiMM will call 'C'. Now, comes the matter of roads behind Ross Station, the extent of which is curtailed by the presence of the cattle-pens and large water tank. Some imagination is required to accept the presence of four additional running lines, but it is necessary to provide. substantial non-GWR orientated accommodation for the 'foreign' companies also represented in the setting of a considerable array of appropriate signals.

This arrangement will also meet Michael Aslanian's view that the trains should be visible from the body of the Centre and provide an attraction to visitors to ascend to the Gallery. Basically, there will be two pairs of double-track roads capable of being divided into three six-foot lengths by section switches. Therefore, in theory, up to a dozen complete trains could be drawn up for viewing behind the Ross setting; this being especially desirable in a display which must be unattended for a substantial part of the time the Centre would be open. The author considers that this area should be handled by a separate controller, which we will call 'A'. So, at this stage any rate, the whole display is divided into three horizontal bands, 'A', 'B' and 'C'. How this will work in practice remains to be seen. This is Sunday morning, 27th September 1998, and my youngest granddaughter is pulling a wooden train, loaded with soldiers, into my study. It must be in the genes this tremendous attraction for the species 'railways'!

Noting the numbers of supply points to the tracks required from each controller exercised the need for a 'busbar' type connection board on the shelves. These have now been made from a three-eighths inch thick, by 1 inch by 7 inches wood strip, with a chocolate bar type connector block at each end. Between the blocks are two lengths of 2mm copper wire which comprises the busbars. The complete job is screwed to the inside of a date box with sides pierced to allow for seven pairs of wires to the tracks. The wiring will be soldered along the busbars at a one-centimetre spacing. If even more 'feeds' are required, then these might be obtained by seeking the other connections below the baseboard and tapping into these in parallel.

On 6th October 1998 the writer received a letter from Quadrant of Cleobury Mortimer, near Kidderminster. This was from Robert Colquitt, a director, to whom my letter to the Newport plastics company had been passed. Included was a quotation for fitting 4mm cast acrylic screens over and around the RiMM baseboards. Today, the 7th, we met at the Antiques Centre, Ross, and spent an hour measuring up and deciding the finer points. Interestingly, he suggested that the straight sided cabinets should have a sloping roof, from front at eighteen inches high down to about sixteen and one-half inches at the gallery rail. This scheme should 'lift' the viewpoint so that it is not disturbed by reflected light; at the front edge the transition will be a moulded curve from vertical to the 'roof' angle. The turntable screens, he felt, should be some fifteen inches in overall height, giving fourteen and a half inches clearance overall – this should just accommodate the mechanical coaling plant at thirteen and a half inches – the highest item in the collection. We worked out that locks for each of the 6ft sections and one for each of the divided turntable 'lids' should be satisfactory. Robert anticipates the job should take until about the end of October and the cost is £1,000 in round (quite large!) figures.

The second week in October also saw a visit from Mr Stringer of NFU Insurance, asking if I would value a pensioner's collection of 00 railwayana. I agreed rather promptly, being accustomed to occasionally valuing such items for Michael Aslanian. However, I was more than slightly horrified to take delivery of three massive cardboard boxes – full to the brims! About a week later, I produced two sheets of computer output listing over 100 units of railway model 'history' – from about 1959 to 1980! How glad I was to have kept catalogues of the period but it was surprising to find, say, that a new Hornby 'Duchess' costing £4 1s 6d in 1959 would cost anywhere up to about £60 today, i.e. fifteen times as much!

I found that to take 50 per cent of a 1998 purchase gave a basis for valuation although inspired guesswork has a role, as is the location of Ross for limited sales potential and, where I know so, the comparative rarity of such items as a 3-car Blue Pullman from the 1971 catalogue. I await the reaction of the anonymous pensioner to the prospect of getting about £600 for his collection – if he can find an outlet. Mr Stringer left with me the few items in which I expressed an interest for RiMM. railway signs, and some buffer stops including a lit version I need to replace a time-expired item for the Monmouth Bay. I was fascinated by an excellent

Hornby tanker 'Traffic Services' No. 4679, which carried the anchor sign associated with stock suitable for train ferry services and operation on the European mainland. It is a remarkable piece of work, particularly in respect of valves and overhead access. To date I can trace no details of the prototype although the model was catalogued in 1964. The other piece of rolling stock which caught my eye is the Hornby model of the toilet and stove fitted LMR six-wheeled passenger brake van HD 4076, also catalogued in 1964. I already have a slightly improved version on RiMM so I turned to the Southern Railway files to seek a suitable van from that company or its pre-Group operators. I turned up drawings of a South Eastern & Chatham six-wheeled covered carriage truck, which promised an interesting conversion.

I have not previously given a detailed description of a 'conversion' from a particular RTR model, but do so in the above case. Having discovered a reference at page 136 *et seq* of David Gould's booklet *Carriage Stock of the SE & CR* and the drawings in *Railway Modeller*, October 1980, by Terry Gough of the CCT in later days, a start could be made. The drawings were photocopied by daughter Susan onto a sheet of 130 gsm smooth cartridge paper. This gives an inner outline for each side, plus an outer version from which the panelling can be cut with a scalpel. The rounded corners are knocked out with a one-sixteenth inch leather punch.

After tidying up, with a rat tail file, the inner side is coated with wallpaper paste and the panelling gently placed in position. Leave at least 24 hours to dry if you use this method. The other tasks are set out below, with a circle at the beginning; when a tick is added this signifies 'job done'. The listing is simply in the order the work comes to mind and tackled in whatever order appears convenient, but the presence of the list reminds one on returning to the model at any time of what remains to be done.

Conversion of HD six-wheel LMR passg. bke.
to SE & CR 1904 CCT:

- Prise off corridor conn.
- File off all roof vents and stove pipe.
- Fit phosphor bronze spring under centre axle.
- Cut off batteries.
- Make and fit vacuum cylinder & rods.
- Nip off coupling vertical arm.
- Fit two grab rails to each end.
- Fit two horizontal brass rails to sides.
- Add paper door straps at ends.
- Brass sides grabs and handles.
- File off end detail HD body.
- Make & add 8 door hood vents.
- Bend off HD buffer beams.
- Replace with HD 6w d Palethorpe buf.bm.
- Make and glue in coupl. hks.
- Cut off centre brake shoes.
- Add lip extensions to roof ends.
- Add lamp brackets on end flaps.
- Add end doorstops each end.
- Make and add full length footboards.
- Score clear plastic to represent early glass louvres fitted to side doors.
- Drill and cut out area around new windows, remove old glazing.

Although it can scarcely be seen, the ragged cutting out of the last items was touched up with dark cream paint. The brass handrails, l4mm pins hammered for door handles, were attached through the sides with Evostick; the surplus bits being nipped almost flush at the rear. Before adding the plastic 'louvres' the frames were coated with shellac and, when thoroughly dry, painted with Humbrol 133. When all dry, the glazing was Evostuck into position. This is my usual technique for coaches and means that the top coats can stop clear of the glazing. The planking on the end doors was scored with a scriber and paper strapping, doorstops, two grab handles, and a rear lamp bracket to the near side added.

Each end of the van was padded out, in card, to match the overlap of the new sides, allowing the new ends to fit between. Most carefully added is the approximately 5mm of extra roof length, carefully bent in plastic and with tiny scraps to match the existing guttering. The continuous footboards are drawn out on tinplate, back to back, with holes drilled to match the position of the axleboxes. These are then filed to an oblong shape and the boards cut apart along the top edges. The L-shaped hangars are cut from computing wire, and hammered flat where they will be glued to the HD solebar. Solder the hangars to the metal boards first, offering the whole lengths in position. Nick the tops of the axleboxes to act also as a gluing point.

Check that all the handrails, eight-door vents etc, are in place before shellacking the body sides and ends. The 'lake' SE & CR livery used is Gloy LMS Crimson Lake or equivalent, the lettering deep yellow. There is a grey chalkboard at each end. This outline of the work involved in a relatively simple 'conversion' does represent considerable effort, but the pay-off, with a simple light phosphor bronze spring lightly bearing on the centre axle, is a vehicle incorporating the best of HD engineering below with an unusual historical body above!

The last dark days of November 1998 are with us now and only the middle of the days are kind to modellers. Looking at the items I had been given in exchange for the valuation, the author settled upon a heavy box containing a 3-piece casting of a typical Southern Railway prefabricated concrete footbridge by Hornby: No. 5010 in 1960. This good model required only a little 'dirtying' along the lower mouldings and khaki on the steps. The bridge number plates are cut from brass and a couple of old "Southern" posters were unearthed and mounted on a card base, adding authenticity to the whole scene to which a mother and two children were added. Whose enthusiasm for railways did not start by peering over a bridge across the lines?

Further discovery was a rare Hornby kit (R 076 of 1982) which had long awaited assembly. Research produced photographs and drawings of this elegant, plastic latticework footbridge – virtually identical to that built by the Rose Street Foundry, Inverness. The writer decided that Highland passenger paintwork would be more appropriate than the Hornby green and was quite fascinated by the improvement, together with painting the steps khaki. The maker fitted a most attractive shield trademark to the sides of the footbridges, above the tracks. These were reproduced by folding a scrap of brass, holding in pliers, and with a rat tail file, finished both in one go with scalloped edges. Details of both contrasting footbridges, together with magazine references to the photographs and drawings, are given in the *Railways in Miniature Museum* catalogue. Almost 400 items are listed and the exhibition, even when models are static, is well worth a visit. The model of Ross Station is the centrepiece, together with a wide range of pre-Grouping/Grouped locomotives and rolling stock from 1880 to 1947.

The first of December 1998 was indeed a day to remember, for Robert Colquitt of Quadrant arrived with the huge drum-like plastic covers for the turntables at each end of the RiMM baseboards! With much appreciated help from the Centre staff, we got those 58in diameter 'wheels' up the two sets of stairs to the Railway Gallery, where they were screwed to the edges of the turntables. The overall effect is quite striking although the centre pivots will need strengthening.

The acrylic sections for the straight sections arrived with Robert on Thursday, 10th December – a rain-swept morning and there was nothing for it but that the writer helped him to carry each of the 6ft sections inside. Anyone thinking plastic would be lighter in weight than glass would be rapidly disillusioned as it has to be remembered that these sections have a 16in rear section, reinforced with thick material. The horizontal section (the lid!) 6ft by 2ft 6in, contains a hinged part six inches from the rear, so that a 2ft wide strip lifts for access; to this by a heat-treated 15in return to the vertical is the protection from hands frontispiece. All in all, a really difficult job to carry around corners and up two flights of stairs to the Railway Gallery!

We set one of these 'covers' in place and juggled it gently over the gallery edge where it rests against the baseboard. A row of pre-drilled screw holes await the fixing, but will need someone standing on the steps below to put the screws in. We shall put a couple in first, aligning the curved sides of the turntables to fit at both ends of the outer sections. Adding the centre section would complete the coverage. Robert had provided drilled blocks at the top rear of the covers, which can be bolted together to secure the whole job.

The author has recounted the foregoing in some detail in case anyone following is tempted to see this work as an easy option! Each of the 6ft sections has a lock at the front edge for security of the contents and Robert has provided two wooden struts for each to support the covers in the 'open' position for access. Setting all this in place is something not possible single-handed, due to the Gallery's location, and the author has asked Haydn Robinson, Serena's husband, to help with this task.

Beginning to see the time when visitors will be asking to enter the Gallery, the need for a catalogue becomes more urgent. Happily, it is all in the author's computer, but needs editing and general tidying up, which, hopefully, Serena and Haydn will undertake early in the New Year, 1999.

Monday, 21st December 1998 was the red letter day when Haydn joined the writer to set up the acrylic covers. Initially, it was necessary to replace the West End turntable pivot with a steel tube and coach bolt. Hardly had we seen the light with this problem and checked that the East End pivot had already been similarly improved by Matthew (at Kemp's), did John, my other son-in-law, arrive with his case of tools! Between their energetic endeavours, covers one, two and three were rapidly raised into position and Hadyn's great height (6ft 4in) enabled him to reach the screw fittings facing the 'auditorium' where the congregation used to gather. The boy (the author !) went out for brass screws for this purpose and also, on John's advice, managed to buy the last two four-outlet electrical sockets from Woolworths. These he fitted with incredible speed in the cramped conditions with the baseboard cabinets and all tested satisfactorily.

Serena distributed sandwiches and we worked through until after 2 pm. The author had failed to find suitable anti-static polish for the covers, but John discussed it and we thought a 'car' shop might be the answer – and so it was. The swept out and polished cases really looked good and, initially, we now contemplated cutting an inch and a half off the West cover to get a closer fit to the turntable; the East End being alright. However, Haydn says it will be simpler to extend the baseboard to fit rather than risk damaging the acrylic covers. This task awaits his availability. Meanwhile, the writer has begun to sort out track for the West End turntable.

This will be single-line with a point off at each end to serve additional two sidings on either side. These will accommodate mainly static display of, say, four engines, but, due to limited line length, more likely showing freight and non-passenger rated rolling stock rather than bogie coaches. A new 36in radius Peco point, with built-in sprung Electrofrog, will be at each end with a bulb in platelayers' cabins. These will light up when power is reaching the track as a visible reminder to operators. The two sidings are controlled by old fibre based points modified in the author's usual manner, which is with one-sixteenth of an inch slivers of phosphor bronze soldered under the running rail and on which the point blades engage and carry the current. Two elderly hand levers are mounted on one-eighth inch ply to allow for the raised track upon foam strip ballast. Before laying, two sleeper centres were cut out to clear the head of the centre pivot coach bolt and a similar gap cut out of the ballast strip. This is to give access to the bolt i.e. by releasing the nut below and knocking the bolt upward just sufficient to allow insertion of an oiling rod.

First use of the power supply was to heat a low-wattage soldering iron to joint the track; this with .029 copper wire with omega loop to allow for expansion and ensure better continuity than the usual sliding fishplate. Thursday, 31st December has arrived and it is good to look back on 1998 and record even the slow progress of the baseboards, but a variety of extra items of buildings, tunnel and rolling stock have usefully occupied the writer particularly to suit the most unusual arrangements we have had to adopt to function in a narrow gallery.

The author has to live with the need to take a couple of hours sleep during the day, but hopes to spend mornings around at the Antiques Centre in 1999, using the afternoons to write up the work sheet etc for next day. It is remarkable how one misses use of a bench vice and the afternoon sessions at 'Chase Side' do allow preparation of such items as the brass finger grips the writer has designed for easier lifting of the acrylic sections.

Yes, 1999 represents a substantial challenge but the author is glad to be here so to deal with. It is heartening to record John's reported remarks that he is "most impressed" by what has been achieved to date! So far, so good – we might say!

CHAPTER SIX

Millenium Ahead:
1999

T he first week of January 1999 found the writer spending two hours each morning from 10.30 on, or rather right underneath, the left-hand West RiMM show case. This was used as the work bench for the West End turntable for one centre track and the sidings earlier mentioned. Even for January, the mornings were incredibly **dark** and, on Mary's advice, a little lamp with a computer disk shade was transferred from 'Chase Side'. This revealed that the rapidly vanishing Jenolite anti-rust liquid, used for fifty years as soldering flux, was running out... Mr Parker got me a pot by the same maker, but it is plainly a new mixture and rejected its role as a flux! Happily, another jar of soft soldering paste appeared – made in Illinois. This is as a grease in application and lacks the speed of a spot of liquid.

However, work is now proceeding and the omega loop track joiners are effective. The author also bent up, from lin brass strip, two finger grips which fit under the front edge of the acrylic covers over the straight cabinets. This makes opening and shutting down possible without trapping one's fingers. Most of the joints around the West turntable main track, with two sidings, involved each section being lifted over the 15in high acrylic barrier on a sheet of Perspex! This is an awkward, wobbly process since the ballast strip has to be inserted underneath. Some omega joints broke in the process and remaking them is like working in a glass bottle – most difficult, especially with the slow flux. Both ends are wired for underneath current collection and a platelayers' hut contains a Hornby 12v coach bulb; hence, when current is applied to the turntable track a light in a hut each end will glow and warn the operator that any engine present is likely to move!

Some lengths of copper fencing, recovered from the old outside circuit at 55 Keston Road, are located either side of the trackwork, leaving about 30mm gap. Into this, and also on the non-railway side, the writer is preparing some 'rough grass', being strips of felt carpet underlay split into two layers. This is sprayed with artist's varnish, to set the vertical strands, and finished with Lada Summer Green car spray. On Monday, 11th January, Haydn joined the writer and, using an experimental burst of anti-insect jet in a water spray, recleaned the acrylic covers to an almost perfect shine. It all looks very good. He extended the No. 1 straight section basement by one and a half inches to match the running edge of the turntable, and the writer looks forward to laying the two 'back roads' and seeing how good (or bad!) the alignment to the turntable centre track turns out to be.

The two points on the West turntable are worked by hand levers from the old layout, mounted on quarter-inch ply plinths to allow for the depth of the ballast foam. This is extraordinarily difficult in the tower-like space. Two half-inch countersunk screws hold the plinths in place, on which a further two hold the lever. Preventing the point from moving is by half-inch steel panel pins through holes drilled in the centre of the sleepers. Only two per point are necessary. Indeed, these nails are necessary to penetrate the MDF board; brass versions simply fold up.

By Friday, 22nd January, the felt strips either side of the fencing are in place using PVC glue and, joy of joys, next day the author collected 500 ml of Baker's liquid flux from the Broad Street Car Shop. He also dawdled long enough to search through their vast range of 72nd scale aircraft kits for a Westland Wessex which the GWR used in the early 1930s. No. such luck; but the success of the liquid flux, put on with an old paintbrush, really made a difference to work on the rearmost tracks on No. 1 straight baseboard.

Next week the furthest track, No. 1, was laid along the baseboard rear and connected to the busbars linked to 'A' – the left-hand H & M controller. The first couple of yards, approximately to the baseboard join, were interrupted by isolating switch No. 1, to allow the 'holding' of a train if required. These sections' switches would be fitted where the point alone was not sufficient to isolate a train-length holding track section; the rail **furthest** from the controller being always that interrupted. On Tuesday, 26th January 1999, the author put the North British tank locomotive on the back road and turned on the controller for the first time. It moved nicely and was probably seen by visitors below.

This simple operation gave the writer some joy and confidence that his wiring was logical, but that the pencilled plans must be carefully followed, particularly in the matter of double-rail breaks upon the point exits where power was also supplied from the other end of the layout. The 29th of January brought the invoice payment for £198.91, to NFU Insurance for the models; although no more than a couple of small models are in place on the baseboards, the 'Wilton Castle' and the 'Mail Coach' need the cover.

The two pairs of tracks against the gallery rail are now in place and the wiring, after much crawling beneath the baseboards, is now looped on to cup hooks against the underside framing. At least this arrangement means that alterations are simple and if the baseboards are eventually separated for moving, the coloured wires should guide rejoining straightforwardly. The next pair of tracks are the GWR 'up' and 'down' lines through Ross Station. The 'up' lines include a 3-way Peco point, introduced to reduce space needs, the nearside track serving the cattle pens. This point is an Electrofrog and complex in external wiring – difficult as the drawing provided is a view from under the baseboard for fitting electric motors, whereas the author needed a bird's-eye view to suit overhead mechanical operation.

Consequently, uncertainty followed the wiring up and a low powered test with the tank engine produced a sudden fast run which negotiated the 3-way and ran on to the big West turntable before running on to its 'dead' rails! Lucky in every way!

As the tracks move slowly across the straight baseboards, it was quite critical to transfer the lines on the drawings onto the base and to remember where the matter was left the day before. In fact, the author has a clipboard of daily notes to guide the next day's work and sometimes to do some 'home work' in the afternoons. The exact location of the Ross goods shed became important early in February 1999, and the writer twigged the method a lady would use i.e. make a paper pattern outline. This was done by splitting open A4 used envelopes and drawing around the bases of the goods shed, Ross Station buildings, footbridge and signal box. Drawing pins hold down the corners and have proved an easy way to avoid damaging the actual buildings at track laying stage.

Both Ross water tank and cattle pens were laid in place complete to aid placing the tracks within the limited depth of the baseboard, the author feeling that the station forecourt will be much nearer the viewer than with the previous arrangements at Keston Road. This was inevitable since the quadruple back 'roads' of the new display had not earlier existed, but were essential to give some scope for running the non-GWR trains within the view of people in the auditorium of the Centre – as was also Michael Aslanian's wish.

The necessary wiring for the 3-way point, with the Peco PL 13 switches upon the baseboard top, needed concealment and the author built the shed associated with the cattle pens. Putting in the 'up' track No. 3, from Hereford and the 'down', No. 4, section from Gloucester were connected to controller 'B'. The latter track included the single-slip giving access to Ross goods yard. The trackwork in this area is necessarily simplified and the headshunt, extending to the West turntable edge, had to incorporate a small radius Setrack point in order to divert the line around the goods shed site. In this area, hand-operated point levers are in order, and the very shallow ballast in the coal yard was replicated by using the 2mm foam from an old ironing board cover.

Monday, 22nd February 1999 saw the successful wiring of the Peco single-slip from the 'down' Hereford line into Ross goods yard. In view of the uncertainty surrounding this unit the author made double-line breaks with insulators from all four outlets, and connected power directly to the two outside rails. Again, the Highland tank engine swept through with aplomb! The back roads, against the cabinet rail, received dead switch treatment, 5, 6 and 7, so that trains up to six feet long can be held stationary. The maintenance roads, two connected to controller 'C', were installed to the left with both lines ending against the West turntable. These would be switchable as appropriate. Each of these roads would take half a train, tipped up on double width ballast sponge for adjustment, oiling etc, within easy reach of the operator.

March saw work proceeding to the rear of Ross Station and the actual main building is in approximately permanent position. This enabled the main lines to be set up and the connections to the 'up' lines from the station rear to be laid out. Directly behind these are the four extra running lines, the nearest serving the cattle pens and spaced to allow for the major water tank – for so long a landmark in the area. Work was now moving to the centre and right-hand cabinet, setting the rear tracks first. A *Railway Modeller* small advertisement resulted in receiving a perfect, mint condition Gem 12 lever frame, from a Dr Chalmers of Grimsby. This is for the 'East Box' in the right-hand cabinet and another dozen levers are a likely requirement – but, goodness knows from where. The writer rather dreads having to make them at 'Chase Side'!

Jeremy Whitehouse, one of the local artists, dropped in to invite the author to a showing of his railway paintings in the Ross Heritage Centre shortly. He was quite interested in the model buildings although they stand higgledy-piggledy among the rails. The writer thought the projects contrasted interestingly in style – his in two dimensions – mine in three; both relying upon photographs taken thirty-five or so years ago! Later, John, Susan's husband, phoned to invite me to select one of these paintings for myself! Such a surprise, but it will be nice to replace one of the WVR wall-pieces which will be going into 'store' at Rowberry's following our 27th March 1999 board meeting, all being well.

Work on the trackwork leading to the Ross engine shed and Monmouth Bay is proceeding either side of an early Easter. This involves scrap brown envelope base patterns for the shed and the tunnel, which will conceal the auto-train departing for Monmouth. The track laying must stop short of fitting buffers due to the need to place a length of plank to lie across this area to support sections of track assembled for the East turntable and representing a joint Grouping locomotive depot.

Despite scale drawings, 3 inches : 1 foot, of the layout the writer was surprised to see how 'tight' would be the fitting of the tunnel (long enough to take the auto-train) between the rear corner of the engine shed and the right-hand baseboard, abutting on the East turntable. Similarly, the lengths of a storage 'road' behind the tunnel had shrunk to room for nothing more than a single locomotive or 'failed' piece of rolling stock. The reason for this seemed, at least in some respect, due to the space required for the points available without opportunity to use a 3-way space saver as laid at the Hereford end.

By the close of March, the final four-inch sections of the running-rails, which would connect with the East turntable, were in place. Wired back to the 'A' controller's busbars were the four rearmost roads. The 'up' main to Gloucester and the 'down' line from that city were wired back to the 'B' controller. The idea behind putting a deliberate short 4in section at each track end is that this is a handy size to replace if any snags develop. Connections directly back to the controllers are in heavy single copper, which was selected to be available for this purpose. It has the advantage of apparently maintaining these up to about 18ft long without discernible voltage drop.

In April 1999 the writer added green grain-of-wheat bulbs across the controllers' busbars. These light up immediately a controller knob is turned and are most useful indicators seen at a glance. If there is a 'short' on the track there will be no light as the controllers' thermal cut-out will be tripped out until the problem is removed. If an engine hesitates for any reason, the bulb will flicker and draw attention; when it runs steadily this will be reflected in less current to be shared with the bulb in parallel, but it will remain alight. The writer temporarily avoided fitting the buffer-stops on the Right sections in order to allow some flat assembly space for the East turntable tracks.

But, the first task was to mark up and stick on the paper tape, which would safeguard drilling and sawing at the entrances in the East turntable plastic drum. This went surprisingly well, using the cardboard tunnel pattern to draw around as used for the West version. The 13th of April turned out to be a lucky day, because Haydn was able to give a morning's work to RiMM. He made an exceedingly tidy job of cutting out and sticking down the 'grass' for the Railway Air Services airfield in the East turntable. The other half of the surface set alongside two sidings was likewise covered for any additional displays e.g. to display a variety of full size railway items such as whistles, watches, timetables etc.

The author decided to experiment with a technique of increasing the length of the main line, through the central pivot, by 4mm extension at each end of East turntable 'through' line. This should enable the inevitable deficiencies from exact 'roundness' of the turntable drum to rotate clear of the connecting ends whilst the track ends are as close to each other as is possible. It will be interesting to see whether this works in practice! This turntable also has one half of its surface 'grassed' by Haydn for varied exhibits in front of two display sidings.

Under the turntable bases, the three-quarter inch sections of broom handle were stuck with builders' glue, at about one foot intervals. This provides simple finger grips with which the turntables can be both rotated (and stopped!) with considerable precision. We are still awaiting the means of supplying power to the 'tables, via plugs and sockets, when suitable items can be located.

Over Sunday, 18th April, the day before my dad's birthday, the writer redrew, for about the sixth time, the motive power layout for the East turntable. The aim is to provide, in the half-disc space, reception of engines via coaling plant, ash pits, water cranes, then a choice of coming 'on shed' or turning first on the Hornby table. The latter is much altered from out-of-box condition; mainly by repainting but, also the control cabin recovered and with vacuum operating equipment added. It appears quietly convincing. The plastic moulding, which includes the gearing and motor, has been modified as to access for greasing etc.

The writer had acquired eight Hornby Dublo cast buffer stops – some designed for 3-rail operation and another three fitted with red grain-of-wheat bulbs. The rail clip wires were bent down to dig into the sorbo ballast; not without some difficulty, the plastic buffer heads on the electric versions were wrenched off, the sleeve reduced and Evostuck back in place. Touching up with silver paint and with Humbrol 26 khaki over the glossy grey frames reduced the toy appearance and heavy construction designed to stand juvenile handling. They look very businesslike for the motive power depot and an illuminated version is reserved for the Monmouth bay at Ross.

May 1999 saw some six months' work by the writer, every morning, six days per week, laying the track within both big turntables and through the three straight cabinets. From 4th May, the left-hand cabinet was opened up and the first set of lever frames screwed on to the 7in wide control ledge. The first shock (always something!) was that the six-track roads were quite close together and in places had insufficient clearance for all signals without gantry provision. However, the first was a splitting Midland Railway item for the far tracks. Thus began the unpacking of the one-sixteenth inch copper tube and the two coils of steel wire, believed to be of 22 and 24 gauge. At the underbaseboard point an upturned L-shaped bracket, 15mm 'leaves', was drilled and snipped to receive the tube end to which it was soldered.

Should you, good reader, employ a similar technique of underbaseboard soldering, do take care not to be directly under the fall of hot flux and solder! The wire fitted into the simple rocking-lever, which penetrated the half-inch thick baseboard. Again, this is folded up from tinplate (empty steel oilcan) which is 15mm wide and 30mm long, bent at right-angles in the centre. The lever is cut from brass, drilled centrally to take a drawing pin and 15mm apart with holes to take the operating wires. The drawing pin is the pivot and, with a thin paper washer in between, it is soldered to the vertical flap of the rocker – simpler to make than describe. In a Treetex type baseboard, a keyhole saw slot is all that is required, into which the rocker plate is pushed. Evostick under the horizontal section will set the job firmly in place. The steel wire is greased as it is fed into the tube and the inevitable friction depends upon the diameter of both tube and wire. About four feet is the maximum length practicable between point or signal and the lever frame.

At the frame another problem may present itself upon a 50 per cent likelihood basis! It is that the lever in the 'at rest', or unpulled position, should hold a signal in the 'on', at danger, position; on a point the lever at rest should set the road for the main route. This arrangement is tested for immediately behind the lever frame where, by putting the wire in pliers, it can be operated and the point or signal watched. With the Midland splitter, one arm obeyed the 'at danger' rule with the lever at rest, the other behaved in opposite fashion! This is a problem solved by putting a horizontal brass plate, with holes 12mm apart for the wire and a central hole to take a screw through a 4mm collar, which mounted behind the lever, reverses the movement at the other end.

The first point to be connected, a Peco on a curve, also needed the horizontal rocker treatment; these points are spring-loaded and quite a pleasure to connect. But, the work was to be quite suddenly interrupted on 11th May 1999, when Michael Aslanian announced that he wanted to talk to me the following day. It was difficult to prepare for this, but the writer noted a few points which might be raised including my advice to 'appeal' his community tax, about the seats being upholstered at the rear of the gallery, my outlay of over £3,000 to date, an estimate that by mid-August we should be able to open, but could meanwhile invite donations via my 'Engine Front' box.

Next day, Michael indicated he would **not** appeal against the tax increase; did not want the seat upholstered in case sitters damaged the windows; he put little faith in possible August opening, concentrating on his estimate that half of the cost the presence of RiMM to his business was £3,000 for this year starting January 1999, and £3,600 from January 2000! The writer said there was no way this sort of money could be taken as donations from visitors and guaranteed overall by a commitment by the Founder. Thus an unacceptable proposal faced RiMM, which the author took to the family on Thursday, 13th May.

Serena and self held a council-of-war and we agreed to explore alternatives. So it was that later that day the writer was found crouching on the floor in W. H. Smith's seeking railway magazines in which the sale of RiMM might be advertised. Suddenly, Serena appeared and said, "Come away – problem solved!" She led the author around to Rowberry's in Copse Cross Street (our Wye Valley Railway Registered Office) telling the writer that she had earlier, by chance, met with John Gartside, who had enquired as to the RiMM situation. He immediately offered the space the Bison glue company had earlier rented and both she and the writer collapsed into armchairs in his room in considerably shocked appreciation!

This space is just about the same in length at 28ft, as the Antiques Centre gallery measured, but the width is some three times more at 20ft 6in. The scope is, therefore, quite outstanding and will need much consideration. The following day the author returned to the Antiques Centre and told a quite gobsmacked (no other expression seems to fit!) Michael Aslanian that regarding this matter, as he had earlier said, there was nothing personal – simply we face an incompatible situation of an 'arts' matter in the impossible context of meeting even half of an assessed 'commercial' valuation. Indeed, money is the root of all evil and although we all need enough cash to get by it has never been an out-and-out priority in my life.

The author has since written to Kathy Gee, the Director of the Regional Musuem Authority, explaining our dilemma and referring to the £3,000 required this year, and the £3,600 for next. The letter also indicated the availability of Serena, a registered disabled person, but capable of tutoring etc the RiMM project and that we are seeking another venue rather than selling up. Response is awaited.

Meanwhile, it is arranged with the Centre that RiMM will be removed next week, and the writer has begun to bring delicate items home, unsoldering track sections crossing cabinet joins, cutting the cables between the cabinets and bundling the ends with string. It is not so destructive as might be imagined and, as the family feel, the Founder will not be under such pressure to press on as at the Centre... Maybe a cup of tea will also be on offer!

Tuesday, 18th May 1999, found John, Haydn, two of Rowberry's mechanics and the author, at the Antiques Centre for a 9.30 am start. Michael Aslanian let us in promptly and the team rapidly knocked off the wooden trim which lined up and locked the cabinets together. It was decided to remove the heavy cast acrylic plastic security covers from the straight cabinets to reduce both height and weight. We also released the round drum turntable sectors, but had to leave the plastic circuit in place. The main casualty was the toppling around of the trackwork within, for since it was on 'MDF' board, no pins were possible – only the electrical wiring held it lightly in place. Although the author had unsoldered or pulled off insulated joiners, the track breaks did not precisely 'fit' the now detached cabinets and some damage, both to track and points, resulted.

However, with the help of three cars, roof-racking the turntables on Haydn's, all was taken around to Rowberry's and unloaded into a room 28ft by 20ft 6in, reached by one flight of moderate stairs; all completed in two hours! The author looked around in some amazement at the size of the space and the possibilities. There are no windows because of the difficulty of changing an old building originally believed to be a store for sheep fleeces. However, one has to accept that sunlight is an enemy to artificial creations and the reason why large parts of museums, art galleries etc are lit with considerable care. John spoke of availability of colour-corrected bulbs and the writer explained the need to show the railway liveries as close to the originals as possible.

John produced a most useful connection box, by Honeywell, which would be ideal to restore the wiring between the cabinets. By a strange coincidence, the 28ft width of the new area was very close to that of the gallery at the Antiques Centre. However, because of the new **depth**, it was possible to ditch the problems inherent with the huge turntables, leaving about 18ft of straight cabinets and then bringing together the six lines at either end into simple double-track which would **circle** the room! This new scheme is on paper only in the week ending 22nd May 1999, but it is a nice solution offering the prospect of some continuous movement on occasions. The writer will need to adjust connections to the controllers as it will be necessary to have two separate circuits, 'A' and 'B', in order to run 'up' and 'down' trains at the same time. Only one engine-in-steam was the limitation at the Centre.

The writer established that the three straight cabinets, 18ft, run, with Ross Station central, would fit across the back of the room; four feet from the wall containing buttresses about 15 inches deep. At both ends these cabinets would be 4ft 6in clear of the side walls, and new sections would bring the six-tracks into double-tracks for the circuit. The points would be finger operated, at least at the beginning of operations. Serena rapidly sketched a reduced 'oval' for this, which could be contained in a 6ft 6 inch space to the rear of the main cabinets. This has the advantage of not being pierced by any of the three doors in the room and so avoids temporary connections in lifting sections. As this is written, we have yet to align the cabinets after the move, but the Honeywell 16-terminal boxes are in place ready to receive the bunched cut-ends from their neighbour.

In the last week of May 1999 most points and signals on the left-hand cabinet are connected to the levers, the 3-way splitting signal at the Hereford end of Ross Station responding to the gentle action of Duckham's engine oil lubricated levers installed in the West end frame. Very pleasing to the writer since it was all of thirty years since they last worked at Keston Road! Geoff Gartside visited to see the sights and seemed quite impressed to see the central, mainline, 'board' come off so smartly from the remote lever frame. Yes, the author mused: this work is going to come as a surprise to so many, both to local people and visitors.

It is pleasant to have members of our family dropping in at Rowberry's and today, 7th June 1999, found the writer connecting up the Ross cattle pen line to the 'up' Gloucester road and lever frame. Geoff appeared again and helped to move around and align the three cabinets. West left, Ross centre, and East right-hand, into a line-astern arrangement across the width of the room with a 4ft rear access corridor. With 2ft 6in deep cabinets this brought the front edges out to a 6ft 6in mark within which a double-track circuit, oval in form, could be formed running through Ross in both directions.

Work continued on re-soldering the track across the centre, Ross cabinet, and early June saw the connections to the 3-way point and single-slip in place. At the Hereford end of Ross is the 'starter', a modern version with subsidiary to the goods shed. This signal stands **on** the down platform so it is necessary to start building now. Collecting three-quarter inch thick scrap timber began for this, when topped with some one-sixteenth white card, built up to the right platform height, 3ft to 3ft 6in above rail level. Remember to allow for the depth of model ballast used; one quarter inch sponge in RiMM's case. The writer had prepared some paper cladding to represent the concrete slabs, but the contractor at Ross had incorporated much horizontal brickwork and appropriate 'papers' have begun to be laid with cellulose paste.

At home in the afternoons, the writer was inspired to build a structure which would be called the 'Gartside' viaduct as a tribute to the family which has found RiMM a home now. Delving into the scenery files revealed a host of civil engineering features from which a six-arch, two-track example would emerge. The base is a piece of ICI Perspex, 28in by 8in, upon which the structure, cut from quarter-inch ply, stands. Cutting out the arches involved using a junior hacksaw blade set across a 12in jig-saw frame. The arches themselves are 'lined' with half-millimetre thick card glued to the pillars. The 'river bed' is contained in a shallow box, three quarters of an inch deep, on which suitable pebbles are glued and **varnished**! Daughter Serena advised upon the green and blue paint added to a crumpled piece of kitchen aluminium foil, which forms the river bed and is allowed to sparkle through. Standing upon my workbench at 'Chase Side', the work is shown to non-Gartside visitors(!), has found general approval and gives the writer some satisfaction. Creating something out of very little has long been my joy!

By 20th June 1999, the author had arrived at the time to fit the 'down' starter bracket signal to the frame. This was significant since it is mounted upon the platform and so began Ross passenger station base from scrap wood topped up with fine white picture framing card. A card guide was cut out to demonstrate the height of platform and distance from rails. This is a simple tool and avoids repetitive measuring. It was with a feeling of some delight that the signal was fitted and both it and its high-mounted ground signal (for goods shed access) were connected to the lever frame. Such memories flooded back as the brick paper and home-made 'concrete' slabs were laid. The two end loading bays for scenery, traffic, motor cars etc, followed and the platform level taken gradually down with card sheet to the baseboard front, the level at that edge being three-eighths of an inch (about 10mm) above the ground level to avoid too great a slope.

In order to follow railway practice, that signals and points in the lever-at-rest positions should be 'on' and 'main line' respectively, the writer has found that about eight out of ten connections had to have the horizontal 'rocker' (previously described) in order to obtain the right lever position. The 3in deep cross-bearers below the baseboard virtually dictate the direction the tube runs take and this becomes expensive in the use of both tubes and the fine wire within to the extent that it is necessary to obtain more of each! John (Gartside) produced, within 24 hours, copper coated mild-steel wire as used for mini-welding processes. This seems to do the trick – perhaps the copper-cladding is stiffening it near to the springy steel used earlier. The writer got in touch with Mr Conroy, of Co-Bra Tubes, Tipton, for a repeat order of ten two-metre, one-sixteenth tubes and these should reach RiMM by the end of July.

Searching one day for something else, my tools and materials spread over twenty feet of bench-top, the remains of two previously made bridge crossings came to hand. One comprised only a pair of ancient Triang lattice girders and the other the deck of a lower Lydbrook cylinder type viaduct handmade some thirty years ago. In afternoon spare time this July, these have been rebuilt in great heat up on my landing workshop. Today, 10th July 1999, the outside thermometer reads 90 degrees F and the writer must keep out of the sun now in Britain, which shines, despite continuous pollution clouds, with African fierceness. The Triang girders now span a road in which two bus stops appear, hopefully awaiting some suitable 'loaned' vehicles. Both it and the cylinder viaduct are spaced to take double-track on 3ft radius curves and will provide some interest on the lines either side of the Gartside viaduct.

Searching the garage for 'deck' ply the writer chanced upon a very battered and chipped mirror which has provided a nice base for the 'cylinder' version which, immediately identified so by Serena, has aluminium tablet containers from Superdrug, instead of being cast iron as the original! Continuing at Rowberry's, the 'up' platform base is now in place together with the splitter 'bracket' which is the starter to Gloucester and Monmouth branch (the latter seldom used by this route) and stands clear of the platform. To the rear is the exit from the cattle siding, but this proceeds ahead to give extra 'loop' space as well as a return to the 'up' main line. This needed a 'bracket' rather than the original single home signal, and the author has utilised the example of the earlier 'down' starter displaced by the 'modern' version just installed at the Hereford end. The next excitement was dictated by the need to accommodate another platform erected signal, the 'starter' in the Monmouth bay. Some of the wood base already in place for the main station was painfully chiselled out to allow the Dublo electrically lit buffer stop to fit. Then, using the bay platform awning pillars as a guide (no closer than 24mm, equal to 6ft) from platform edges, the under platform wood strips were screwed in place. The 'new' 1937 built signal box stands at ground level and has access steps to be built around it. Before any detailing with this proceeds, the bay track, with engine run around, was added and connected to the 'C' controller.

The writer received a copy of *Railway Modeller* for father's day, from daughter Serena, and by mid-July had found time to begin to read the advertisements! Much to his amazement, Hornby item R 4095 is a 68ft LMS six-wheeled bogie dining car – long wanted for the RiMM 1930s built LMS train. Dapol had produced such a model retailing at £25 in 1987, which seemed too much at the time. Comparison with a *Model Railway Constructor* photograph in June, 1987, and the new model, which Totally Trains supplied, indicates an identical first/third composite at £14.75. Apparently, this model began life under Airfix, was marketed by Dapol and 1999 is made in China (!) and retailed through Hornby!

On the bench the diner interior needed some additional detailing – providing the writer could find the way in! Careful feeling around at solebar level indicated sufficient 'give' between the one- piece sides and roof as to allow a fingernail to be drawn along and the sides parted from the solebar and underframe. The three side mounted clips, which held all together, were sawn through and discarded. They would do pushed back without such fixings as the author would need to access bulbs etc. Originally, the solebar section was offered by Dapol either with or without a gap immediately above the six wheels to give clearance on tight radius curves. The new model was the gapped version (no alternative being offered). However, it was not difficult to fill the gap with plasticised card strip and Evostick. More comprehensive brake rods were added and the Triang type coupling prised off. In this section a 4mm length of one-sixteenth copper tube is glued vertically for the author's own coupling to drop in. The tables now have aluminium foil cutlery, various blobs and plates of 'food' and the tablecloth white paint is extended down the sides and ends. Slater's plastic people are painted and have menus in hand; two standing figures operate in the kitchen, two standing stewards have loaded aluminium trays and are shown serving passengers.

Having discovered W. Hobby Ltd as a source for dwindling numbers of 3.5v bulbs, at a modest 31p each, the usual four were wired in series in the diner with the phosphor bronze socket towards the engine. At the far end fine jumper leads in copper flexible wire are soldered to 14mm pins. The latter await a Bachmann LMS 'Open' third to deal with the diner overflow.

At Rowberry's, points and signals to the East and West continue and nineteen of the twenty levers in the right-hand cabinet are in place. It must be admitted, no tears will be shed when this 'wire in tube' work, so much being under the baseboards, is done. Today (29th July 1999) the outside thermometer is 91 degrees F, and inside 'Chase Side' and the garage it is 71 degrees F – still very warm to work.

Later, on Monday 16th August, the second batch of one-sixteenth inch copper tubing is still awaited, but the time has been absorbed in cleaning through the track above all three straight cabinets. Inevitably, a few of the connections between cabinets have been wrongly reconnected, but the writer has cleared controllers 'A' and 'B' circuits of which the former operates the 'up' main (and extra back roads) and the latter the 'down' main and Ross goods shed etc. Circuit 'C' includes the two maintenance roads on No. 1 (Western) cabinet and the Monmouth branch and associated lines on No. 3 (Eastern). The 20 volt bulb and leads quickly identified the few faults and the gallant little North British tank sped along in confirmation.

The task which proved quicker to execute than anticipated is the painting in white the numbers of the signals (red) and points (black) levers. Each of the three lever groups is numbered from one onwards, including the white 'spare' levers numbered in black. A diagram, of white cardboard, now lies in front of each lever frame. This is simplified (as the real thing) but clearly shows the location of each point/number and a sketch of each signal/ number. Additionally, the operational location of the end of each of the sixteen ex-RAF 'dead' switches are shown on the diagram by a green square with the appropriate number in black.

The latest (and last!) batch of one-sixteenth copper tube arrived yesterday and today, 20th August 1999, saw the first of two last remaining bracket signals – an LMS upper quadrant example, installed at the extreme East end of the lever operation. The one remaining is the GWR Monmouth splitter, either to the Bay platform at Ross or on to the 'down' main where water can be taken. This represents the end of the lever frame connections for signals and points; the rest at each end, where the double-track oval will run down each side and complete the circuit along the

28ft rear wall, will be hand-operated. Life is simply too short to consider further lever frames by this writer!

Beginning to set out the West curves quickly made it apparent, even with the track rescued from the now obsolete huge turntables, that a substantial quantity of new track is needed. Double-track means double the money expended (as the full size railways know!) and a couple of Peco 5ft/2ft 6ins points-on-curves will be purchased in addition to a box of 25 Peco Universal wood sleepers track lengths. The writer, and occasional family and other visitors who can't resist the open door, have remarked on the beginnings of the 'oval' and the three viaduct/bridge sections, as bringing the work to life as a display of potential to a considerable range of people. From 'Knit and Sew' of Cheltenham, came more quarter-inch thick foam for ballast: ready-cut 46mm wide strips, requiring only trimming off the edges to represent the ballast shoulders – an excellent source and most reasonable in price.

By mid-August, track laying for the West curves (Hereford end) began to hit the inevitable design problems of merging the six tracks on the straight baseboards into the double-track circuit. This meant alterations to the original, which are in pencil (a good tip!) so can be altered, within an outer radius of approximately 3ft 3in down to about 2ft minimum. However, tests with the 70ft 'Wye Valley Railway' van and two six-wheel bogie Caledonian coaches proved the practicability if coupling spacing and speed (!) are carefully controlled. A variety of set-curves are to hand and these guide the process of avoiding over-tight laying. One regret is that the Peco point-on-curve is 5ft outer radius; no doubt less is impractical, but 4ft would be more convenient. Several straight section points are incorporated and these seem to enable the locomotive to regain a little speed after tight curves.

Using tight curves means drilling one millimetre holes at about 4in intervals through sleepers and inserting 1in pins. Not very 'prototypical' but quite necessary to fix through the sponge ballast into the insulation board. As each line reduced itself to the double-track circuit the author tested the electrics by each controller and the 20v bulb unit. All was well and the North British tanker rode well on a short freight train. Moving across to the East 'return' lines, in mid-September 1999, the writer began testing with the 20v box. A distant rumble hit his ears and he was only just in time to prevent the freight train vanishing off the end of the Western lines on the far wall!

Passing Ross Station front it was noted how the congestion around the East end of the goods shed could be relieved by taking about 7in off the nearest 'maintenance' siding. Removing this allowed the coal merchant's stables to be moved aside and this simple adjustment much improved the overall setting. Perhaps, this is a good lesson **not** to do too much detailing about goods yards etc, until the whole 'vista' emerges.

The Eastern return has the additional interest of accommodating the LMS/LNER flavoured locomotive depot. This includes a substantial (18in long) engine shed of Midland origin, and LNER wagon-tippling coaling plant and the modified Hornby turntable. Currently, several versions of this corner of the layout have been juggled to fit the limited space. This is being aided by a double-slip, a quite marvellous creation by the Peco engineers, which gives maximum flexibility in a difficult situation. The points in this area being hand-operated from the front of the cabinet, means that the matter of reasonable reach becomes paramount. However, the basic 'through lines' of 'up' and 'down' tracks will be the normal setting.

The heart of the East End, bringing the six tracks into the double-track circuit, centred on the beautifully made double-slip by Peco. Once again, moving from the maximum radius of 3ft, inwards, with each addition reducing gradually, to serve the ex-Midland Railway/LMS engine shed, the LNER wagon-tippling coaling plant and the much-disguised (now 'vacuum' assisted) Hornby turntable. Out with pencil and rubber, the final layout is emerging this September – which has simply flown by. Because of difficulties of stretching the human arm sufficiently(!) it is desirable to have some points lever-operated, although on the prototype hand-working around the sheds was the rule. The writer is trying a new supplier for any extra five-lever frame and the outcome is awaited.

Meanwhile, the opportunity is taken to run 3 and 6 volt DC 'mains' under the basement for buildings and signal lighting. The buildings include the new 3.5 volt imported miniature screw bulbs (from Hobbies) and some 2.5 volt torch-type bulbs. Usually, all are wired in pairs in series, to reduce brightness and also to increase bulb life. Granddaughter Michelle visited today, but cried rather than switch on some lights! Never mind, the author worked the switch and her eyes and Susan's (mother) opened wide to see the little magic show. Doing this work gradually will enable the odd single lamp to be allocated to best advantage between lighted buildings.

The 6 volt circuit is to work the Hornby bulbs in the GWR Ross signals; the bulbs in the buffer stops being wired into the tracks so that they only light when an engine is on the circuit. The wiring of the signals is arranged so that the tipof the bulb is fed by an **insulated** wire. The phosphor bronze clip which holds the body of the bulb being soldered to the metal dolls and posts. It follows, that since the operating tubes/wires are soldered through the signal base, that a connection simply to the tubes will complete the circuit and light the bulb. The matter to watch is that the insulated wire (orange in this case) **always** goes to the bulb tip; the wire to the carcase/tube being black. With three lever frames it is just as well to solder the black lead to each tube near each signal. This will reduce checking elsewhere if a bulb fails to light.

The flex carrying both 3 and 6 volt lines has a 2in square heavy card disc every five feet. These contain four holes through which the flex passes and is soldered to two copper clad sleepers, which act as busbars feeding adjacent buildings, signals etc.

October 1999 finds the writer finishing the hand-operated points at the extreme ends of the main baseboards. An attempt to use a five-lever Masokits frame, built up from brass etched sheets, proved abortive in the context of distant operation. More practicable for use as a ground-frame, perhaps with shorter runs, was the verdict. Looking at the three completed frames, totalling 59 levers, the author feels that it is a case of sufficient-is-the-day-thereof! If some other hands care to extend the remote switching and operation of the rest of the signals now in place – all well and good.

Meanwhile, most of the 'static' signals and points are set to reflect 'normal' settings and so will not require continuous adjustment by the signal person. Ross Station area required the addition of black 'spear' fencing and this is, fortunately, available

105

commercially in either brass etchings or (cheaper) Ratio plastic. Fill-in scenic strips of three different short grass sheets were added and rough grass, represented by old carpet felt, dabbed with a grass green water paint. The station 'apron' and other tarmac areas were painted with flat grey oil colour to which, when thoroughly dry, khaki was added along the edges where dust naturally gathers, and also drawn to represent the country tyre marks from road traffic. White builders' adhesive laid on with an old paintbrush secured both varieties of imitation grass, pressed down well with fingers. Brown paint is gradually applied to all pin heads fixing sleepers and the omega loop rail joiners, with khaki on the card barrow way and the 'lids' over screw heads at point rockers.

By the end of October 1999 the author was working to lay the part grass, part hardcore of the Railways Air Services area. This had occupied a half-section of the West turntable at the Antique Centre so considerable change was involved. Incorporating the 'modern' SR prefabricated concrete footbridge, various wheeled trailers etc, the Little Staughton control tower and the wind-sock blowing in the prevailing wind, the whole is now satisfactorily awaiting the first aircraft! Then RiMM received an invitation to participate on a course: 'Display and Interpretation for Smaller Museums and Heritage Attractions', from the Hereford Council. This required payment of £50 per person and was to occupy four days, ending at 2 pm, at Ross Heritage Centre. The author thought it worthwhile to offer the students a view of RiMM under construction, later that afternoon. This was accepted by Ian Standing, the Community Heritage Officer.

However, this invitation posed some dilemma of providing at least some locomotives and rolling stock before we have dealt with security matters. Nevertheless, with Serena's help, it should be practicable to bring in and take away afterwards some items. Looking out several trains, the author decided the 1914 Royal Train carrying the Duchess of all the Russias back home might be appropriate. Then the World War I freight train could demonstrate something of the awful things to come. The rest would be the Monmouth 'bullet' auto-train and a 3-coach Hereford – Gloucester GWR passenger train, hauled by 'Torquay Manor' as the writer remembered in 1938. It will be interesting to see how many turn up and what reaction occurs...

However, the 'best laid plans of mice and men do often go astray'...
On the day before the visit was due a message was received from
Ian Standing to the effect that the students would be too tired to
appreciate RiMM, but would attend at some later date. At this
time of recording, 14th November 1999, we have heard nothing
about the grant application made on 28th July for financial aid
for RiMM. The writer fears that, without even a site visit, the
Council has made up its mind to turn down that request. Since it
had not even acknowledged receipt of the twelve pages of forms
submitted, as is the normal practice of Hereford authorities, it
was unlikely to advise us of the outcome! The embarrassment
of 'using' RiMM's facilities for course members was something
they would avoid at all costs!

On 8th December 1999 Ian Standing took me to a meeting of
the Museum Forum at the Cider Museum, Hereford. This was a
pleasant occasion where we sampled cider currently made, up to
and including a most potent brandy fortified version! Some of us
raised the matter of no reaction to the grant applications we had
made in September. A response was promised and duly arrived
– RiMM and five others being rejected. We were considered
among the most varied collection of 'Voluntary Sector' people
including Much Marcle Parent & Toddler Group. Highest sums
were granted to a Music Audit operation(!) and the Leominster
Money Box Credit Union! The writer feels RiMM and other
museums should **not** be considered among such a miscellany of
purpose to share the derisory sum of £12,925! I will be writing to
the new chairman, Dr Noel Meeke, of the Hereford Waterworks
Museum, explaining that unless we are properly recognised
and considered under designated budget within the Arts &
Cultural, we will withdraw from the Forum. Further, the writer
expects the previous aborted application to be transferred within
that process **and** that the assessors should actually **visit** RiMM
for, incredibly, the 1999 decision has been taken in Leominster
without even a visit by the officers concerned!

Thank goodness the author can continue setting up RiMM in
a practical way; the most important as December romps by, in
the rear section incorporating the Lydbrook type viaduct, the
Gartside Viaduct and the rail over road bridge. Chunks of 2in
thick plastic, cut out by Haydn, provide support for the medium
fibre base. The long spirit level kept the track more or less free of

gradients and it was, with great pleasure, on 1st December 1999, that the author coupled the North British tank engine to the little goods train on the 'up' line. It steamed out of Ross with more confidence than I dared to have – and was soon around and over the viaducts with steady determination and soon appeared as a train from Hereford into Ross. Very satisfying! The remaining signals, to be non-remote controlled, were spaced out along the back roads; located by their catalogue numbers also on their bases and site places. The signals joined the telegraph poles in boxes to await the erection and painting of the scenic background.

In the last week before Christmas 1999, Haydn began a stint with me and we arranged two three-drawer filing cabinets against the wall to support the 'Mail Coach' showcase. In the recess, alongside the entrance staircase, we topped over the two wooden cabinets, previously used to support the turntables. These were then ready to support the 'Wilton Castle' showcase. This action really began to 'open up' the central area. The next task was to re-hand the entrance door so that it opens outwards acting correctly as a fire exit. Enormously heavy, it is almost certainly a half-hour fire door. The process went well with two pairs of hands and Haydn screwed the displaced handrail on the door. A hook and eye from Scimitar completed the job, of which Geoff and John seemed to approve.

The next planned item was to saw one of the turntables down the plastic centre in order to make two half-orange shapes as wall mounted showcases. The 2in by 2in plastic bar through the centre was exceedingly hard work – only hand sawing was possible and progress was little more than one inch (25mm) per **hour**! Days later the two segments are apart. On the morning of Christmas Eve, the author cut the under-circle of MDF into four segments and screwed and glued them together as double-layer quarter segments. These would support each half-showcase, in the centre, from the wall, and two extra brackets would take the weight and stabilise each end. We are looking forward to seeing the results. This leaves us a spare turntable, and Haydn is recommending we install a rope barrier rather than reinstate the heavy plastic covers over the three straight Ross Station sections. These were necessary to protect the contents at the Antique Centre because visitors could just drift up there unsupervised. At Rowberry's the door can be locked while unattended.

Upstairs at 'Chase Side' the writer found the two 3ft high 'A' frame notice boards originally used for WVR display. With screw-eyes at the rear these would support the rope barrier in the centre of the 28ft run and Haydn has secured two miniature 'poles' for two ends. Certainly, such 'open' access would assist both cleaning, especially the rail surfaces of the oily black scum which seems to appear – possibly from use of plastic wheels. Meantime, a wooden stick, about 40mm by 12mm by 12in long, has become the basis for an experimental rail cleaner. At the business end, a quadruple layer of cloth is folded under and secured with a couple of elastic bands. A few drops of turps substitute is dropped on the cloth and the stick drawn gently along the track. The scum is easily removed and the author intends to experiment with the method in future – there is mounting pressure, good hearted, that trains run very soon in the New Year!

Serena came in and began sketching the scenery on the background card sheets, which rise some two feet, around the back and side walls. We have in mind filling in the background between tracks with soft-board, with sloping areas around the bridge work, finished off with the various lengths of carpet felt, model grass sheet etc. Ian Standing has asked whether we can "open early in 2000" as they have publicity about to go to print. The author enquired of his colleagues and we have agreed to meet this deadline. We aim to open 10 am to 4 pm on Thursdays (Ross main shopping day) and Saturdays in the New Year. Serena and Haydn have commissioned Mark Cunningham to paint two outside boards to be displayed when we are "OPEN". The author has proposed some alterations including that the word 'Museum' appears rather than 'Exhibition'.

CHAPTER SEVEN

Millenium Modelling - My 75ᵗʰ Year: 2000

T he year started with the author's decision to write to the new County Council nominated chairman of the Museums' Forum regarding the need to have a budget dedicated to the museum cause – **not** to set the requirement among the voluntary sector which includes mothers and toddlers, pop groups etc. Happily, Haydn has been available for several 'January 2000' days. He has varnished the main door and the remaining cabinet fronts. The half-disc turntables have now been erected. One contains the Butcher pioneer aircraft and the other Bert Everall's and the stationmaster's hand-lamps. The latter cabinet will be available for varying exhibits, even any more expensive 'sale' items, as it is lockable. The writer has put in 58in of single ballasted track at the rear of each half-disc. These will accommodate a full train as a static exhibit, for example, a train contemporary to the 1909 aircraft.

The idea of erecting some scrap soft-board to fill in against the layout background painted scenery has been abandoned, because Haydn decided to use the material horizontally, level with the tracks. The author has covered this with variations of the commercial 'grass' mat in hand and, as we reach the end of January, has commenced outlining on the backdrop of 'holly green' (Dulux water colour) hedges up to the West end of the Gartside viaduct. To the East, the fencing has become 'Cotswold' stone walling between the fields. It is in a khaki shade with lighter shade topping stones. Doug Eaton, the artist in adjoining rooms, visited and announced it to be 'very good'; most pleasing, for the Founder is but an amateur painter!

Rolling stock and engines are being moved from 'Chase Side' as family transport is available. This repacking revealed an Airfix post mill kit of 1959, unmade. It seemed ideal to relieve one of Haydn's plateaus and the finding of a Como electric motor, with gearbox, in the garage has made another little project! This is now installed and has a switch in the West control location on the 3 volt DC supply. This reminds the author to record the visit on 15th January 2000, of Lesley and Andy Lowe, of All Components, Hereford. This was arranged because both the 'C' circuit controller, a very early Triang effort, and the Bassett Lowke controller, arranged to give 3 and 6 volts, were quite time-expired. Andy produced the agreed 2.5 amp MPC5/0 gauge controller which we had agreed would give ample power for the long, frequently jointed, track around RiMM.

They also had brought an HH2 handheld controller with which we carried out some satisfactory running with the little North British tank and the Hornby 'Manor'. The HH2 enables one to wander as far to the East as the LMS motive power depot and was ideal to spot the trouble tight curves were causing to 60 and 65ft coaches. The writer decided to put in some 'check' rails on the sharpest curves and the Monmouth line was terminated rather than leave a point at a pressure point. This is quite a useful tip – even if it involves minor rebuilding – which no one is likely to have noticed. However, the usual stock of bullhead rails has been used up for heavy duty fencing etc, and an alternative had to be found for the 'check' sections. This was solved by stripping (with hot soldering iron casing) some mains cable – tinned copper of about one millimetre in diameter. This is soldered at 75mm intervals to 25mm pins, allowing about 1.5mm between check and running rails. This improvement was supplemented by inserting some 2mm card, one centimetre wide, and cut to the same radius as the track bed, pushed underneath to provide superelevation.

This is something generally ignored by small-scale railway modellers, but there is no doubt that tilting the stock a modest amount is most helpful in negotiating tight curves. A further modification that came to mind, remembering that the engine needs steady power throughout tight spots, is to wire (.029) the check to the adjacent running rail to ensure continuity of current flow. Again, this proved worthwhile and on the line out of Ross to Monmouth, is certainly correct to 'prototype' although the tortured squeal of flanges against check rail is missing!

111

At home the writer contemplated, with block sketches, how the 'trains display' would exist in practice. Basically, there should be an operating train on the 'up' road (controller 'A'), on the 'down' track (B) and the Monmouth shuttle as 'C' controller. Immediately behind Ross Station lines are three roads, electrically isolated for three trains on each – nine in all. The cattle pens line will accommodate two trains. Ross had a headshunt both to West and East; these are modelled and provides space for a further two trains. Directly behind Ross engine shed is room for yet another train and the Southern engineers' breakdown train can be housed, even if in two sections, within the LMS motive power depot. Total on display, including two in the half-disc showcases: 20 trains. This fits the original aim of 1960!

The author has to find some £200 for insurance for RiMM at this time. The NFU Mutual has refused a grant to cover renewal and this is being pursued elsewhere – quite a disappointment as RiMM is the only surviving museum project in poor old Ross! Contact with Peter West, Acorn Insurance Group, Sittingbourne, who the writer's wife suggested via an advertisement in *Railway Modeller*, resulted in a good package of cover. This the author explained to Viv Stringer of Ross NFU Insurance and we remain railway enthusiast friends. Nevertheless, the process left the writer £181 to find for the premium.

The telegraph poles and 'static', (but setable) non-GWR signals along the background tracks have now been added. Repairs have been effected to the 6ft table Geoff Gartside has offered and this now awaits the shallow cabinet he gave the writer and is stored at 'Chase Side'. There is a list of items to be moved which will need a heavy lift. The little lathe so seldom used has been given to John Gartside; the heavy 'Ross Signal Box' plate, a section of broad gauge rail and the Wye Valley Railway paper assets moving for storage.

Now into the last full week in February 2000, the author set out a Second World War freight train, largely of USA supplied vehicles etc, together with the LNER O2 2-8-0 locomotive to stretch its legs. This was erected on the 'down' line out in the country on the Hereford side of Ross. Simply rendering the Ross down platform lines 'dead' held the 'Manor' stationary while the LNER freight moved gently away. So glad to have incorporated those l6 ex-RAF switches to control such sections. Almost unconsciously this happy event was paying off and it would be quite practicable to have **two** trains on each 'up' and 'down' line – provided some space was kept between them. This was really only possible with 2.5 amp On Track controller MPC5/0 on each line being designed for 0 gauge and ample power for two 4mm engines. Eureka! – sometimes that which may be blindingly obvious arrives to give us special delight!

With Susan's help, several loads, each of four apple boxes containing engines and rolling stock, have now been moved from 'Chase Side' to Rowberry's together with the 1960s two-road embankment which saw great service at Fairfield Hall. This ups the total static tracks in the half-cabinet from two to four – really necessary since it is now clear it will **not** be possible to show all 300-odd locomotives and stock at any one time. However, the author is working upon a number of **changes** during each year, which are related to important happenings in the real world during the 1880-1947 period, for example, the return of the Russian Duchess on 1st August 1914 at the outbreak of World War I and the vast freight load the British railways carried either side of the 'D Day' (invasion of the European mainland) in June 1944.

Sipping milk on a late February 2000 morning, the author sat down and viewed his 'empire'... He thought of the need to provide something of a 'script' to which a curator could relate without the inherent knowledge of the Founder. This work divides itself naturally into a story to cover the main layout building items. The locomotives and rolling stock visible at any one time would largely explain themselves – especially if a catalogue is purchased. The other talk relates to the contents of the individual showcases around the walls; largely occupied by the large scale, air, water and road transport models – about half-an-hour in all. It will interesting to try these out in due course!

Into March, the writer decided the half-cabinet, originally for 'occasional' items, should contain **six** tracks filled with overfill RiMM engines and stock! The highest track of the Fairfield embankment now carries the 1914 SECR Royal Train. This, with its elaborate, flag decorated engine, is simply too fragile to display on open tracks. Now, it can be viewed very closely, but also in safety. Some 300 engines and rolling stock can now be 'on show' at any one time. The rest are in shallow boxes 'in store' but accessible if we have a visitor with special interests.

Andy Lowe, of All Components, Hereford, has brought in a specially made unit to give 6 and 3 volts outputs each at 2 amps, this to replace the very old Bassett-Lowke item for lighting, windmill etc, operation. This unit has a controller basis and so the voltages are brought in gradually – very sound as this adds to the life of the numerous bulbs involved. He also brought in two identical 2.5 amp MPC5/O controllers to replace the 'A' and 'B' old H & M Duettes with 1 amp output on each circuit. One additional handheld (HH 2) controller on four metres lead, joins the one already in use. These are arranged so that the operator of the 'down' and 'up' roads can move to the extreme ends of the frontage – where the tight curves exist and where any problems can be closely examined with controlled track power.

In effect, at the cost of some £250, the low voltage electricity supply for RiMM has been replaced for the Millennium and, although funded by the writer's pension(!) is seen as a most satisfactory situation. Some cash has already been placed in the 'Eric's Engine' collecting box and the advice that this should be chained down has been implemented. The writer has been painting and has generally improved the look of the central area in the middle of the layout. The two hand-lamps (Bert Everall's and the stationmaster's) have been bolted to two 8in by 10in brackets which Haydn has mounted high above the corners of the half-cabinet. Fortunately, power is available below and we admired the effect of electric bulbs; necessary as it would be too dangerous to light by oil in the museum.

Early April finds the writer wiring up the new controllers and working upon notices etc, which will be required once we open from Easter Monday, 2000. Mary and self will be present for the 10am – 4pm opening on Thursdays and Saturdays thereafter. If we lunch early in town on those days we should, hopefully, be able to reopen by 1 pm. A fortnight ago, Doug Eaton and Christine took on the preparation to publication of the rather enormous RiMM catalogue and guide. Christine extracted my input into this computer on disc and set about editing the contents. The writer was taken aback at the number of inconsistences in detail, especially regarding abbreviations, varied use of punctuation etc, which are regrettable, but almost inevitable in the decade during which the catalogue entries have been added. With the author's marvellous old 1955 Ross Ensign roll-film camera a series of time exposures (1 second at F 11) were taken alongside and overhead of the Ross modelled area. These have turned out rather well and we will make a selection for the catalogue cover and also to accompany some old black and white prints showing how RiMM has developed.

The writer, apprehensive of this venture in publishing, is concerned as to the overall cost and has sent out three 'begging' letters to London Cultural & Arts organisations. It is rather a cart-before-the-horse situation because the author fears most recipients will simply not believe what has been achieved and it will need the actual catalogue to grasp the significance of the project. A costly exercise to provide copies free of charge. Doug and Christine are confident in having some copies available for Easter Monday and these are hopefully anticipated!

Haydn came in on Monday, 3rd April 2000, and together we purchased some blue rope and fittings from Parker's ironmongers. These we assembled with two A frames and uprights at either end to form a light barrier between general visitors and the rather accessible models. The writer was able to 'whip' the ends of the rope to the fittings in quite a professional manner. I am not sure whether Haydn believed that this technique was part of the Radar Mechanics' course in the RAF in 1945! He neatly repainted the radiators and we both concluded that his contribution to setting up RiMM had been most effective – pending the arrival of the signal box nameplate etc.

As matters turned out, the 'heavy' lift has not been possible before Easter, so the large table is decked out with magazines etc, offered to those who make donations. Most happily, Doug Eaton and Christine have presented 25 copies of the RiMM first edition 390-item catalogue in time for the Easter Monday opening. Our press release duly appeared in the *Ross Gazette* together with Serena's photograph of Geoff Gartside and the writer; this picture being in **colour** – the first I can recall in this paper! We have decided to charge £4.80 per copy of the catalogue to make a modest profit on the sale of 250 copies at a cost of £927.

The date is now 20th April 2000, and it is Thursday – my last day of structural/setting-out work on RiMM. The feeling is one of having done my best over the year since installation at Rowberry's began. This afternoon I slept solidly for three hours (twice usual nap!) but awoke feeling really rested and generally confident for Easter. The bank holiday Monday duly arrived and the writer hung the RiMM 'OPEN' notices out in Rowberry's yard. Starting was slow and not until after 11am did visitors begin to arrive. Although the author had scripted a talk-through, reference to this quickly proved unnecessary because much was repetitive despite the need to 'fit' the reaction of visitors according to age, whether local, or visiting. The time really flew by and I was relieved by Betty Gartside coming in with some tea about three o'clock, but she was taking it away about 3.45 pm before I could break off and enjoy it!

About forty to fifty people appeared, but my idea of keeping a five-bar gate record failed before it had begun! Two of the catalogues were bought and quite a lot of cash rattled down the chimney of 'Eric's Engine'. There was no press, politicians or other media cover and the writer was glad of this. Until more curatorial folk are available then the casual trickle of visitors best suits the situation. The first Thursday and Saturday followed. Mary joins me on Thursday when we shut for an hour and go down to the 'Rumble Tummy' for lunch. On Saturdays RiMM is the only place functioning in the building so I take sandwiches and Mary has now also been present. The museum notice saying 'The RiMM is full; please return at the time indicated by my detached clock face' is working well.

Gradually, as time allows, the coaching stock with corridors is being fitted with my version of the knuckle couples; dozens having been made during May. Sometime later the pipe-type coupling, dropping into one-sixteenth inch tube, will be tried for the short, non-corridor stock. It looks so good, but the test is ability to negotiate the ups and downs of trackwork and the tight curves. The balance of the 250 copies of the catalogue has been delivered – seven sold to date.

One has gone to Kathy Gee, Regional Museums; another to an earlier grant supporter of 1997; and others to the universities known to have railway or transport study courses i.e. York,

Sheffield, Cardiff, Loughborough, Aston, and Swindon New College. The letter invites visits by students during the summer. As these notes are typed up, on 9th July 2000, the author has to report that not even acknowledgements have been received from any of these recipients! Serena says this is par for course for these institutions. This may well be so but, what price **education** in the public transport field for the new century!

At Rowberry's, on 19th May 2000, the Founder sought to make a soldering repair on a curious catch-you-out brass device brought in by a colleague: the Fly Fisherman. A broken brass tube, mended by a collar of copper wire, had my old Solon 65w iron applied to it, but the iron clicked twice and then expired. The attempt to dismantle it to fit a new element was in vain; the entire unit was welded solid. At Parker's the nearest replacement, a 40 watt Weller iron, cost £14.99. The Solon was purchased about 1940 and had worked so well for **sixty years**! It may defy logic to grieve over the passing of a mere electrical device, but that iron and the Founder had lived together through thick and thin – deriving so much satisfaction from the finished products that it is almost impossible to describe. So long, Solon, rest in peace!

By the last week in June, the knuckle version couplings were generally installed including the rolling stock in store beneath the baseboards, due to lack of display space. This included the 6-wheeled vans. On test some of those had insufficient play in the Hornby centre axle – due to presence of footboards etc, but others were quite happy to be pulled around the circuit by Midland tank 16440, which has replaced the splendid tour of service which North British No. 471 has solely undertaken for track testing since 1997. The author oiled, greased and cleaned out carbon dust from the latter and she runs as well as ever, being 'retired' to a little quiet shunting on the maintenance lines C1 and C2.

It is pleasing to note, by July 2000, the gradual increase in visitor attendance, which we attribute to circulation of the 'flyers' by Mary, Serena and self, to hotels, shops, library, Tourist Information, Heritage Centre etc. It is a great help having Mary present on the Saturdays although it was after a Thursday opening that the first £10 note was found in the collection engine! The Founder became engaged in exceedingly sensible conversation about the 'big one' (Wye Valley Railway project) with a gentleman who, as we glanced through the WVR Feasibility Study, said that he works for Cass Hayward (our original consultant) currently! Not until 4.35 pm did our discussion cease – with their grown-up son crawling (with permission) under the baseboards and engaged in electrics/operational discussion with the writer. We will keep in touch.

Equally, out of the blue, appeared a middle-aged couple, both displaying an unusual grasp of the work displayed by RiMM. Eventually, they introduced themselves as 'drivers' at the Pendon museum started by the late Roye England! The wagon loads here were announced as fully detailed and beyond anything they displayed. Very pleased about this, the writer explained that Roye and himself knew each other and of our aims although we never actually met – other than by phone and letter. Never mind, I am sure he is with us all in spirit. Both they and the Cass Hayward visitors seemed very vague as to how RiMM's existence had come to their attention – nothing like a little mystery in life! We have exchanged a bundle of 'flyers' from Pendon with ours – which should be good for business.

Looking through wagon records at the end of July 2000, the writer discovered drawings and a photograph of two further Forest of Dean collieries wagons. They are Lightmoor and Speech House. The former is a seven-plank with wooden solebars, the latter having six-planks on a steel underframe. Some juggling with Susan's computer produced 'sides' to 4mm scale on cartridge paper. This is stuck to 1mm card with white glue. The 'wooden' underframe is RiMM's last white metal casting of about 1947! The metal version is folded up from tinplate with both buffer beams cut from copper clad sleeper material. The writer has no rail-soldered to copper clad sleepers track and it is difficult to speculate how this would fare if we had used this technique. The summer of 2000 has been highly variable in temperature and although Rowberry House is thick-walled (with **no** windows at RiMM!) it is noticeable that the track pulls up on its 1in (25mm) sleeper pins quite often! This is not serious as the twice-weekly track cleaning shows up the 'proud' examples by catching in the rag – loose pins are simply pushed back. This movement, combined with the omega loop soldered point rods, seems to ride out the temperature variations very well. However, the writer is far from certain how stuck down/stone dust ballast with no flexibility would behave.

On Saturday, 9th September 2000, the author knows not why precisely, but he was triggered by 'brain' to contact Mark Daunter, who lives on the fringe of Ross. He had earlier expressed interest in RiMM so the writer telephoned him saying that we would keep open at least to the end of September. He said he would come in during Saturday morning and did so accompanied by a mounted railway poster of Ross and a timetable of excursions to Tintern in 1878. Also, in marked contrast of styles, an enamel 'Ross on Wye' nameplate in chocolate and cream of Western Region, British Railways. Very quickly we adjusted the available wall space to accommodate these items – feeling that a new dimension had been added to the RiMM display.

Luckily, Saturday morning attracted visitors elsewhere (the local Industrial Steam Locomotive works was open) and we crawled about the layout, giving Mark the opportunity to 'learn the roads' and something of the spiel the writer gives to most visitors. Mary and self retired to the 'Rumbling Tum' for lunch and Mark took his turn on a bookstall at the Market House as earlier arranged. By 2.30 pm we were all back at RiMM and visitors poured in – keeping everyone busy all afternoon!

The 2nd of October 2000 found the writer in overalls and crawling under the baseboards. The aim is to work through the three lever frames, oiling and greasing the connections, pivots etc. A few of the underside copper tubes have become disconnected, but the comparatively simple acts of resoldering the tubes to the tinplate brackets below has restored operation. Such repairs are about 90 per cent successful but one is contending with friction, due to little general use once the levers are set up for the two main circuits with the appropriate signals 'off'. The most important check is that current is being carried through the joints properly, that visitors can see the routes **are** correctly signalled, that engines carry appropriate headcodes (lamps or discs) and that the tail vehicles always carry red lamps.

On Saturday, 7th December, visitors were in the minority so Mark suggested we check operation of the turntable. The writer was

119

surprised to find this inoperable from the centre switchboard! With the aid of the 20 volt bulb-in-box, we traced the faults to two links on the very old (1960 vintage?) insulated frog points. Simply, the soldered joints had broken. Renewing these, the table started to revolve on its own as the lever was 'on'. When all is considered, autumn – as the author believed, was Edward Beal's idea so many years ago – is a good time to add 'maintenance' to the general round of cleaning. Investigating the 'Schools' engine cutting out on Hereford line out of Ross seemed inexplicable. We tried the original North British 0-6-0 locomotive earlier used to test the track and it ran through without a tremor. Examining the 'Schools' indicated a continuity problem between engine and the powered tender. The loco coupling is relied on for one side of the motor current. Further, Mark found the bogie wheels, which occasionally left the track, had been set too wide apart of the axle! Never mind – all sent to keep us busy!

Although it is now November 2000, we are still open on Thursdays and Saturdays, greeting more visitors than reasonably expected. However, there is a change in consist, as the Americans say. Most are local and at least 50 per cent are more interested in the prospects of reopening the Big Railway (i.e.the Wye Valley Railway) than looking at what we have lost through the models..! The two interests are clearly linked and it is fair comment to say that the presence of RiMM has concentrated many minds as to what has been **lost** by the missing Big Railway. This is particularly relevant to the current Ross and District residents, many of whom have moved here in the past decade (HR9 Postal Area now includes some 15,000 people against 5,000 when the lines closed in 1965) and were used to rail communications.

Most Saturdays Mark (Daunter) takes home a RiMM engine for examination, cleaning, oiling, greasing and any adjustments necessary. This pleases the writer greatly for we are undoubtedly running the trains, or rather allowing visiting children to drive them, much more than originally envisaged. However, providing good maintenance is carried out (RAILTRACK please note!) all seems satisfactory considering nothing is brand new! Quite frequently track cleaning will reveal a fault to be repaired. Undoubtedly, the comparatively stable temperature of the room does still vary sufficiently to test the ability of the Omega loop joints to cope with the considerable rising and falling of the track.

This despite 1in (25mm) pins through the sorbo-underlay into the baseboard. Had the track been glued down on a hard base, with, heaven forbid, granite dust ballast, there is no doubt that some bursting of connections would take place and constitute a continuous problem.

On 2nd December 2000, Totally Trains in Ross had arranged to show a large layout at Larrapurz Centre. We noted this in the local paper and ensured that the Centre had some of our 'flyers' in the foyer. The result was beyond expectations and it was a Saturday packed with 'spin-off' visitors, many expressing their dissatisfaction with the exhibition by Totally, for which an entry charge was made. The writer quite enjoyed the exhausting occasion, which kept both Mark and me so busy. So glad my mobile exhibiting days are over – it being such hard work – and one is bound to fail to meet some visitors' expectations. As it was put to us, "Well it's an ill wind that doesn't do good to someone!"

Early in October 2000, RiMM had received a visit from the Council's visiting tax officer about the premises. It was a friendly occasion and resulted in completion of a form for rate relief for the museum. This was quite searching, but it worried the writer when a demand for £349.89 arrived for the year 2000/01! Happily, this was explained as a 'mistake' and should be ignored until the County Treasurer has considered the matter. On 15th December a letter arrived indicating that a 100 per cent grant has been given for the year 2000/01. So far, so good. The author feels able to move the 'heavy' exhibits (Ross Signal Box plate etc,) into Rowberry's – with a more permanent future feel for the whole project.

Mark Daunter has continued his Saturday visits to help both on running repairs, arranging train formations and looking after the potential young drivers who turn up! He was working on a 4mm scale GWR 'King' for his father and eventually this was circling the RiMM tracks. The author quite admired this massive Italian built machine, by Lima about 1980, although the real thing was too heavy to be allowed through Ross! Suddenly, he said, "It's yours, Eric, for Christmas!" Ooh, what a surprise! He wrapped it up as we discussed my taking it back in time to Great Western days – from its British Railways double-chimney presence. So, the end of the year finds my little 'Chase Side' bench hosting, in bits and pieces, the Royal "King Richard I"!

The 21st of December was our last official day of opening RiMM for the winter on a regular basis. However, we will open if there is a special requirement. How soon we reopen in the New Year remains to be seen, especially as the author notes the temperature is well below freezing and the ground is white with snow; not the weather for visitors to venture out museum viewing as the last days of the Millennium are accomplished.

In the course of exchanging mutual good wishes with All Components, Leslie and Andrew, the writer ordered another hand-held mini-controller. This was supplied with a special discount and means that each controller has an extension around the rear to enable us to easily recover trains/faults in the circuit. Something else to keep us amused in 2001!

CHAPTER EIGHT

The Year 2001 Arrives

Surely, it never crossed the writer's mind in the 1940s that he would still be modelling on New Year's Day 2001! However, the day found the author noting down the work to be done on the Great Western 'King' to return it to post-World War II appearance. Quite surprisingly, some forty items needed attention with sixteen different paints and varnishes to finish! Happily, the engine has its main handrails as individual runs, but on cab sides and the tender new steel rails are needed. Lamp brackets, vacuum hoses, whistle shield, fire irons, couplings and lead above the tender motor are in place. The cab has been detailed with reversing gear, damper levers and crew – the fireman holding a GWR pattern shovel from the F. J. Roche most useful drawing of 1948.

Two slabs of lead in the boiler roof, together with a one-millimetre brass contact strip on the centre-driver tyre assist with the one-side motor pick-up on the engine. The Lima safety valve is replaced by one in the 'spares box', although this had to be cut down to the Roche drawing. The major problem of replacing Western Region British Railways 1957–8 double-chimney in January 2001 was that it proved impossible through the retail trade to secure a single 'King' version! Even the enormous advertising content of the current *Railway Modeller* failed through many telephone calls to locate one! Although the 'old hands' understood the writer's problem for an item easily available forty years ago(!) it was plain that 'Ready to Run' is the situation today. In effect, complete 'Kings' are available but **not** the individual components other than in very expensive kits – into three figures in OO gauge today for a loco and tender. This puts them out of the reach of youngsters; many in ordinary employment; and most pensioners like the writer!

So, the author racked his brains, as did the pioneer model makers of the 1920s and 30s, and studied the drawings of F. J. Roche and J. N. Maskelyne, the latter one-time editor of the *Model Railway News*. Maskelyne had published a large scale drawing comparing the chimney of a 'King' with that of a 1945 'County'; an extract the writer has from an undated *MRN*. Sketches on an old envelope indicated the possibilities of a handmade chimney soldered up from odd pieces, the basic materials being a washer bent to seat upon the firebox, and a brass tube section as the chimney (old immersion heater rod) shaped to 'sit' upon the washer, and at the top a further steel washer; the three items being soldered together with a 25 watt iron forming flanges of solder.

On the real engine, the chimney penetrates the upper flange but on the model the washer does not allow sufficient clearance. The solution is to cut a one-millimetre thick ring, from the chimney tube, within which the cupola (raised rim) sits. It is bent from brass strip and soldered to the ring **away** from the rest. The cleaned-up ring can then be **glued** to the top washer and the copper paint applied. The writer would have preferred a professional job – but, beggars can't be choosers! The amendments/additions that have been made to this elderly locomotive have been much assisted by F. J. Roche's drawings, which included the G coat-of-arms W nine-inch lettering appropriate for the passenger class engines in 1944–7. The lettering and arms are drawn out, lightly, in pencil and painted in pale yellow as a base. The arms are shown in colour in *Our Home Railways* and, no doubt, other, later reproductions. Brushes, down to 0000 size, sable if available, are best and a watchmakers magnifying glass is necessary. Paints are Humbrol and, although transfers are available at a price, the writer gets much enjoyment with hand work. Note that the cab-side lining in Great Western times climbed up over the windows, rather than a simple panel below which the Western Region applied.

After experimenting with various plug-in methods of joining the engine to this particularly solidly cast tender frame, the writer decided a soldered lead would be best. These are made from a length of double audio flex supplied for earpieces. This stuff is **very** flexible and used as a single lead, by twisting /soldering at each end; so providing a reliable means of conveying current from the engine pick-ups to the tender motor. By leaving sufficient slack, tidied up into the firebox space, the engine may be uncoupled from the tender with adequate movement for oiling etc.

On 30th January 2001, at 5 pm, the Aston Ingham Beaver scouts arrived to view RiMM! This was prearranged as a special opening in the 'closed season' for small museums. The leader, Penny Smith, and assistant, Mandy Smith, brought additional male and female grown-ups in to endeavour to control the exuberant pack. These, the writer thought between five and eight years of age, seemed more like slippery eels as they rushed about the space, climbing on the seats etc! It has to be said that, apart from couplings parting at speeds equivalent to 150 mph (!), the little lads did no damage. However, an older ten-year-old helping out in the rear circuit space caught his sleeve on some LNER coaches, which fell to carpet. Some electrics in the coaches have broken free and the experimental couplings held together rather too well. Four coaches have been returned to 'Chase Side' shops for fitting with standard knuckle couplings, replaced buffers etc.

Conscious that it is rather too easy to catch clothes in the stock near the inner edge (behind Ross Station extra sidings) the writer decided to construct a barrier which would rise one inch (25mm) high. This has been cut from spare ICI plastic from the 55 Keston Road garden layout. Three strips, 6ft long by 3in deep, have been fixed in place with round head screws into the rear vertical trim. On the facing-the-front side is a one-inch strip of yellow brickwork which gives a nice, light finish from the viewing point. A few poster boards will be added to break the long-run to the front, and some matching paint at the rear.

RiMM closed on 3rd March 2001, while Mary and the writer were taken to a show at Malvern by Haydn and Serena. Next week visitors returned in surprising numbers and the Founder needed Mark Daunter's help on Saturday; his lunchtime employer at the book stall being still on holiday. We had the visitors 'in'as the professionals say, of all ages from about eighteen months to close to eighty years! We developed a technique according to the audience level, which works very well. Mark usually supervises the youngsters driving the trains while the writer 'talks' the others around according to their ages and familiarity, or otherwise, with Ross and its connection with the GWR.

125

On 10th March Mark brought in four 'OO' engines: a GWR 0-4-2 tank, an LNER A4 'Mallard', an A3 and a British Rail 2-10-0, the latter being the last steam engine built at Swindon works. He had been unable to run them since purchase at auction, so it was pleasant for visitors (and the author!) to watch them amble around the RiMM lines. He also brought in a full size British Rail red tail lamp – which quite dominated the exhibits for the day.

Gradually, we are circulating the RiMM leaflets (flyers) around the Ross hotels for the New Year – for the primroses are out in 'Chase Side' garden and the birds are beginning to sing. Despite the terrible foot-and-mouth plague which has hit the countryside, local people are visiting us and we try to raise a smile with them before they face the '2001' world again. On Friday 25th March the Midlands TV and the *Ross Gazette* in the same week advertised the 'attractions' still open in the area including RiMM, and the Saturday following really buzzed with visitors as a consequence! We assume that the Council had instituted this publicity, which falls under the 'It's an ill wind which blows no good to anyone' category.

On Monday 9th April a phone call from Julie Tyler, reporter with Hereford and Worcester radio, arranged a live interview in RiMM the next morning! Both Serena and the writer met her, with her radio linked car parked below. We gathered before the model of Ross Station. Serena was invited to speak and did so very well indeed, relating her experiences as the child of such a railway-mad father! Her present recovery from quite traumatic incidents, recorded fully in my autobiography, is both welcome and remarkable.

Easter seemed to arrive even earlier than ever in 2001 and Haydn and his new Maestro (ex-London Electricity Board!) van effected the 'heavy' transfer of RiMM items from 'Chase Side' to the Museum on Sunday – perhaps the only day in the week it is easy to park there. We took the flatbed showcase, the section of broad gauge rail, map case and the cast iron 'Ross Signal Box' plate. All safely delivered up the staircase and the author is preparing paper exhibits to fill the new table-top showcase.

We continue to receive visitors, despite the foot-and-mouth problem now countrywide. A couple of middle-aged people listened closely to my talk around RiMM, but the writer was somewhat surprised to read their entry in the visitors' book on Easter Monday. The remarks were exceedingly kind and comprehensive – they both hold Doctorates at Cambridge University! This is the highest accolade RiMM has received and both daughters Serena and Susan appear slightly startled at the level of recognition their father/founder has achieved!

We seem to be moving into a succession of three-day openings: Thursday, Saturday and Bank Holiday Mondays! However, although this every-other-day opening is a considerable load, there is no doubt that such Monday openings are filling a gap in places to visit in Ross. Another surprising couple, aged around thirty years, arrived in June and the writer launched into the 'circular tour' of the museum beginning with the ex-RAF communications Anson and Dominie, now representing Railway Air Services of 1946. Mention of aeroplanes as 'kites' brought immediate eyebrow twitching and the author's enquiry, "Would you be in the mob?" meaning the Royal Air Force! They both laughed, the lady producing her identity card as a serving Squadron Leader. It turned out her husband was of the same rank, and it has to be admitted, the discussion widened further than the railways! They seemed most impressed by the Mosquito 'U' Uncle on the back of the catalogue and it's being indefinitely 'on charge' at Wyton Pathfinder Museum.

Undoubtedly, as the founder remarked at the next Museum Forum meeting, RiMM is receiving more visitors than this time last year, but we were only open from Easter Monday 2000, and the publicity in Council brochures was only just taking effect. Experience with operating the layout, particularly by even tiny children, was beginning to need almost perfect running – which is not easy – bearing in mind the **age** of track, locomotives and rolling stock! Inspiration came regarding the extreme right-hand curvature of the line; beginning at the ex-Midland engine shed where the double-slip operates. The writer sketched out some realignment of the 'down' line to eliminate an old point by using the double-slip on the 'up' line and the route out of the slip by a connection which would **increase** the radius of the curve. Mark Daunter agreed and we spent an urgent Saturday morning with cutters, soldering iron, files etc, to make the changes with much merriment and references to the full size efforts of 'Railtrack' as visitors spotted the debris being cleared! Anyhow, all was completed by 12.30 pm and running resumed on both main lines for the afternoon visitors.

August–September saw increasing numbers visiting RiMM although undoubtedly affected by foot-and-mouth disease and then the sudden attack on America on 11th September 2001.

The writer had a real 'busman's holiday' on Sunday 14th October when, with Maureen Tweed, Simon and Phillip, of the Wye Valley Transport Group, he visited the Severn Valley Railway. The writer provided the tickets (shareholders only perk!) and a most enjoyable day followed including a round trip to Bridgnorth and the near vertical cliff railway up to Hightown. The down journey was diesel hauled by a WR 'Warship'. The return was with steam – an LMS Class 5 No. 45110 locomotive – which, on arrival at Kidderminster, the driver invited some passengers and children onto the footplate! What a thrill for several visitors so unused to railways – let alone steam-powered!

Particularly of interest to the writer was the format of the train – almost entirely GWR restaurant cars serving Sunday lunches. We actually travelled in coach 9055 to G43, Lot 1209: a toplight built 1912/3. In 1950s terms we would have regarded it as a 'Nondescript Saloon'. Today, it comprised two open saloons with a first class compartment in between. Our end had double-doors and was likely a guards/luggage compartment with the partition removed. In this condition, wheelchair passengers could be pushed aboard and sit alongside everyone else. The vehicle has been handsomely reupholstered and the writer expects that each saloon would have had a long, centre table in early days. Very many public service buses and a few coaches were also displayed and the whole experience is one which will remain in the mind for a long time. Flyer leaflets for RiMM were exchanged for a batch of Severn Valley Railway publicity.

October 2001 also saw the return of a number of slides Jack Coombes had made from my 200 negatives of Ross Station and area about 1959. He was glad to sell them to the writer together with a projector and screen he had no further reason to keep. The author is rearranging these slides and creating a script so that they may be enjoyed by others. A first showing has been booked for the Transport Group on 17th November. Meantime the writer has built a new heat outlet box for the 300w lamp! Never having seen the photographs so huge is quite exciting – including shots of Mary with Serena in a hired pushchair while we stayed with Bert and Maude at 'Rybro'. Happy Days!

Glad to record that the slide show, mentioned above, went well and some forty people turned up as it had been 'trailed' in the *Ross Gazette*. The new ventilator did its job well and the projector remained cool for the best part of an hour. Visitors to RiMM fell away in numbers, but were supplemented by local people bringing family members from afar who were making annual trips home. Several locals brought in their latest rolling stock and engines. It was particularly interesting to see the latest Hornby coupling, which is a smaller version of the Triang original. The writer must say that had such a neat version been available, it could have changed his mind about adopting a knuckle coupling generally.

Although the present ready-to-run detail in the engines is quite spectacular, there is no doubt that pony trucks and bogies remain the Achilles heel of good running. Certainly, these items either side of often a broad wheelbase of drivers, do demand a very level track, without which the pony or bogie will readily jump the rails. The Chinese tendency to fit pick-ups and leads into the motor from these trucks also act upon easy pivoting and negotiating curves; undoubtedly, 3ft radius is a minimum requirement. Whether or not the track, level when laid, will remain so is much a matter of varying room temperature and expansion/contraction of rails. The writer is pleased that sleepers, loosely pinned to the 6mm sorbo underlay (dress shoulder padding) do absorb considerable variations in movement as happens with real ballast.

Plans to remain open until Saturday 22nd December 2001 were brought forward due to criminal activity locally, and Thursday 20th saw our last opening for 2001. This concludes our first full year of operating RiMM, with approximately 580 visitors, compared with the previous short year of Easter Monday to December, of about 300 attending. There are practical limitations to the numbers of visitors the Founder can reasonably talk through the exhibits and, most regrettably, Cyril Cooper, an eighty-year-old contemporary RAF type, has had to give up his voluntary curating at the museum.

The author adds these words on Christmas Day, 2001, awaiting Serena and Haydn taking us up to Sellack to visit Susan and John, Michelle and Natalie, to exchange presents. RiMM is resting until we begin after the New Year, on Thursday the 3rd of January. Just what will 2002 bring to our little enterprise?

CHAPTER NINE

The Queen's Silver Jubilee Year: 2002

The New Year began early for RiMM and we were open from Thursday 3rd January. Visitors were few in number and local people tended to scuttle in and out of Ross as quickly as possible! However, matters improved steadily, especially on the January Saturday afternoons when local folk arrived with relatives staying over the Christmas period. We closed for the last two Thursdays, when Haydn and Serena took us to shows at Malvern and Cheltenham; the writer needing to rest earlier during those days.

The author removed the Christmas van traffic train, replacing it with general freight for the New Year. The Glenn Miller aircraft was also withdrawn, leaving the Anson and the De Havilland Rapide on the airfield. The Great Western train representing the passenger Gloucester–Ross–Hereford service remained with three coaches, but we temporarily relieved the 93XX. This involved unpacking 'Sir Daniel Gooch', Castle Class, and putting her on the regular run for a while. Although too heavy and wide for the Ross operation, it would be an explainable anomaly! She is a detailed Hornby engine of 1964(!) almost historical in itself, oiled up and with carbon removed from between the ring-field commutator slots, moved off without the slightest slipping with the 'up' passenger to Gloucester. Very satisfying and most attractive to visitors; she is still 'on the collar' as this is written in August 2002!

February saw the arrival of an occasional visitor to the museum and the carrying of an old 'K's' cardboard box which concealed a 97XX GWR tank locomotive. Being of white metal, No. 9789 is probably the heaviest model on the line, tipping the scales at 16 ounces! Lacking chimney and with a curious stub of rod as a safety valve, and also a detached motor, it was indeed a sorry sight. The final insult to the GWR was an ugly cast 'driver' built into the **left** hand side of the cab! After two months' work in the writer's 'spare' time, the various problems have been solved including the break in pick-up continuity. This was cured by adding 1mm strip phosphor bronze strips to press on the tread edges of the centre pair of flangeless driving wheels. The author found that this pair ran a trifle 'high' relative to the outer pairs and as they all pick up current, steady running is ensured. The most fortunate 'find' amongst the engine components at home was a correct GWR chimney! No luck with a safety valve but this concocted from a one and a half inch brass coach screw, cut down at both ends and drilled out for the valves. The gift of tubing from Maureen Tweed's father's collection of metal, included fine tubing (medical injection?) steel, less than one millimetre in diameter; four of which are set in a puddle of Evostick representing the valves.

The addition of lamp irons, tool rests behind the bunker, real coal, extra handrails, top-feed to new injectors plus two appropriately placed crew men, restored the revival. The transfer GWR was correct for the 1940–7 period, but had crumbled through simple old age!

Putting on the goods train at RiMM by early April was most rewarding as she took up the slack and moved off in good style. Almost as satisfactory as rebuilds of the 12in to the foot – full size in the preservation world. She is in direct contrast to 9713, which the author had made in 1949. Time was found to tackle the derailing of the LNER V2's pony trucks. The betterment was achieved in two ways, firstly gluing as much lead into the disused front coupling area and adding a lead block on the truck under the firebox. Checking the height of the check rail on the offending curve by my slab testing device showed the rail, despite being soldered to lin pins, had moved lower, below the running rail level. This was cured by levering up to level and inserting a 4mm length of sleeper, tapered and fixed with Evostick upon the existing track sleeper. This prevents the check rail descending when abused by the track cleaning process.

The latest excitement is, once again, digging out the 'Bulldog' research and contemplating building one as 'River Fal', remembered as a Hereford – Ross – Gloucester engine in 1938! Writing in mid-May 2002, a bright month with lovely working conditions, the writer cut the first pieces of running-plate, the cab and has completed the bogie. Almost surprising is the rate of progress for an engine which is far from simple in structure and therefore so rarely built. One fortunate discovery is that two sets of wagon spring castings in the stock box are suitable for the exposed leaf-springs above the driving wheels and also upon the bogie.

The other key matter is that the Mainline/now Hornby Dean 0-6-0 tender engine has a **powered** tender. This is the 3,000 gallon type and suitable for the 'Bulldog'. This is most desirable because a small motor fitted to a four-coupled engine would have limited adhesion – in such a small boiler in respect of lead weighting capacity. Another real fear was that with putting the power output through the outside cranks of this particular engine, surely the temptation for these to work loose under such pressure is a reality! With a powered tender the writer can indulge in rocking connecting rods to the cylinders, beneath the smokebox and between the frames. An unusual feature would be to fit a Hornby 15v bulb in the firebox and model the door 'open'. Since the tender would be entirely dependent upon the engine picking up current, a glance at the bulb would indicate current flowing.

Adrian, at Hereford Models in Commercial Road, could only supply a complete Dean locomotive with the wanted tender, so the author had to purchase both for £46. Many visitors to RiMM who have '00' gauge models bemoan the extremely high prices of engine kits today; these are close to £100 when wheels and motor are added. Just what proportion of these etched brass kits ever 'turn-a-wheel' as the railwaymen say, is, the writer suspects, probably less than 50 per cent. In order to demonstrate that the most common materials can be used even in locomotive construction, the author has built the boiler of 'River Fal' from old talcum tinplate. Serena has photographed this event for posterity! The running-plate with integral splashers, cut out and bent vertically (avoids soldering and makes a firm base for soldering on splasher tops) is cut from heavier tinplate donated until recently by the car oilcan suppliers.

The major cut-out is made in the cab front which accommodates the brass end of the firebox. This restrains the pressure created by making the Belpaire outline. The cut-out material is saved and has copper wire soldered around the edge to form the backhead. This is detailed with moving regulator, brake fittings, instruments etc, such assemblies being done on the bench and glued with Evostick in position. Time for a commendation to Evostick for producing such an excellent product and which the writer finds improves with every purchase. Always the smallest tubes are purchased as these deliver the tiniest amounts often required in modelling; for example, the firebox doors modelled in the open position have the lever soldered in place, but the item is glued into final position. This avoids the use of multi-heat solder and special irons to avoid assemblies collapsing in many situations on an engine.

It may be helpful to record the uses of Evostick on the 'Bulldog'. These include the chimney, safety valve and piping, the final connections of the driving wheel springs in their brackets, the cartridge paper impressed with 'rivets' (blunt needle) around the smokebox saddle, the bogie side frame and the entire outer frame of engine! The cartridge paper is purely a cosmetic addition to metal sections and painted with shellac, which, together with the Evostick underneath, helps preserve the riveted appearance. Again, this is a cheap way of achieving the effect few can afford to buy a riveting machine etc. The Romford wheels are also treated with Evostick where the round nut fitting is tightened; they will work loose if not so fixed.

We are now into the first week of July 2002, and 'River Fal' is beginning to look rather good in Humbrol's excellent primer paint. The dummy rivets look satisfactory, being such an integral feature of these engines. The driving wheels and the inner heavy frames are fixed to the running-plate by a vertical bolt at the front end, to which the bogie is also attached by a strip of phosphor bronze and a gentle ERG spring holding it down. The rear end is secured by a bolt horizontally mounted through the drawbar. The Hornby 15v bulb is vertically wired onto the heavy frame and acts to show that, tested pair by pair, the wheel set is carrying current for the tender motor and its entire dependence on the engine.

The most difficult part of the 'Bulldog' is the crank on each coupled wheel. This is an Alan Gibson product, tapped to wind directly on to the axle ends. However, it is necessary to have a sleeve between it and the axle. After some experiment the author decided to use a 3mm section of the outer cover of telephone flex. This allows the crank to be wound down to stand clear of the outer frame; both ends of the section being treated with Evostick. The delay in setting provides time to set the coupling rods at ninety degrees to each side; between both sides of the rod holes are tiny washers made from tinned copper wire. The use of a shaving mirror vertically on the bench behind the chassis enables one to judge the opposite rod's position relative to ninety degrees. The outer washer is soldered, through a paper washer to prevent all locking together; an oil-stone block being used to finish off the ends neatly.

The finishing coats of paint – by brush, never having the luxury of spray painting – is by Gloy and some mix of matt and gloss varnish. The aim is to make 'River Fal' look like a working, branch line engine, without exceptional cleaning , but no rust or over-the-top 'dirt' as currently favoured by the magazine writers. The 29th of August 2002 was the great day for the maker and this 'Bulldog' backed down on the Hereford–Gloucester 3-coach set in a most satisfactory manner. It should be noted, for the benefit of future fitters, that tiny coil springs upon the bolts holding both the bogie and tender end coupling are there to ensure **all** locomotive wheels remain in contact with the rails. Since the tender is all rubber tyred the engine pick-ups on all wheels are quite vital. The four driving wheels, to secure the operation of the 'rocking' connecting rods from the eccentrics being between the frames, also need to be in firm contact with the rails.

The author was really thrilled to nudge open the All-Components controller and watch 'Fal' pull away up the bank for Gloucester. Even in artificial light the open-door firebox glows most realistically upon the crew and backhead. Later, a young five-year-old also enjoyed driving her.   The fact that the writer had seen the full size engine at the same place, in 1938, was enhanced by viewing the scene from under the Bay canopy as observed so long ago. Such moments come rarely in life, but sixty-four years on it was all the better!

One of the ongoing problems at RiMM had been the opening up of the buck-eye couplings between the GWR set regularly used on the Hereford–Gloucester service. However, an experiment using a paper clip, half-circle at the rear end of the first coach and connecting with a simple 'L' shaped hook on the next vehicle, seems to have solved the problem. The pressure on the coupling does become quite intense on the sharp curves at both ends of the layout, but the paper clip is both hard and 'polished' so that the freely hanging hook moves freely around the half-circle section even on the tightest curves. The author will watch this operating in practice. With only two clips needed for the 3-car set the bar of the hook is virtually invisible, which is a worthy feature.

Some spare moments during the long summer evenings of August 2002 enabled the writer to sort through some spare mechanisms for possible engines. One such was the Dapol 0-4-2 mechanism. This would be a near match to power a London, Brighton and South Coast engine on two grounds: (i) RiMM has examples of Southern Railway companies prior to the 1923 Grouping, but (ii) lacks an LBSC locomotive. Further, drawings and magazine extracts of the I3 engine are available. This, being a 4-4-2 Express Tank locomotive, would be unique as a type for the museum. The starting point was a drawing by Ernest F Carter in the June 1938 copy of the *Model Railway Constructor*, published from Green Lane, Thornton Heath! Additional help was found and the sources are listed in the second edition of the RiMM catalogue.

As usual, much of the construction is oilcan or talcum powder tinplate with the running-plate support of square section metal from a toy umbrella. The plate was cut out so as to 'sit' upon the Dapol unit as a push-fit. The bogie is of brass soldered to a lump of lead bolted, ahead of the centre point, and connected by phosphor bronze strip to a bolt soldered under the running plate – just ahead of the front pair of driving wheels. This reflects this builder's experience with the 'Bulldog' and others where the bogie needs to swing out beyond the running-plate on sharp curves! The motor in the cab dictates the need to use brass in the near proximity; the spectacle plate being of 1mm sheet, lighter to the sides with built-in door. Frustrated by the lack of copper pipe for the 20mm boiler, a pre-war Corona cigar case of spun aluminium came to hand!

With no special solder available, this might have proved a problem, but Evostick would fix the wash-out plugs and handrail knobs, and make the fixings into the cab front and the smokebox saddle. There is no Belpaire firebox or wheel splashers on this tank engine – a pleasant change from the GWR engines. The saddle is cut from close grained hardwood, held in the vice, and shaped with chisel and garnet paper wrapped around a tube. The piano front, between the frames, and the overlay of the side plates at the saddle, with rivet impressions, are from cartridge paper, treated with shellac. The prominent Brighton works plates are cut from brass, as is the Robinson safety valve, which originated as a hollow rivet. The chimney is of copper tube with washers at both ends; the lower part being shaped to suit the smokebox top.

The dome is a solid block of steel (origin unknown) through which was set a bolt. The latter was held in the drill brace and the dome shape turned with a file; the base being splay-finished with a round file and continually checked against the boiler top. The tank sides are oilcan tinplate being nowhere near the magnetic field. The writer finds it most helpful to cut and try most of the sheet metal work in thin white sections of cardboard first; this is on the principle of measuring twice and cutting **once**, or the technique of paper patterns ladies use to make clothes. Another unusual opportunity arises in the making of the ventilated, raised section of the cab roof. After a lot of thought, this was cut from credit card material at the front and back, as a double thickness; the inner ones being slit to accommodate strips of phosphor bronze as ventilator vanes. The whole is Evostuck together with a tinplate roof over all.

The Westinghouse brake pump, with copper tube sections, is taken from Mr Roche's drawing of LBSC practice and is Evostuck in place. The components are soldered together but without use of special low temperature iron, would surely have fallen apart. Then, of course, it is unlikely a low temperature would get solder flowing on the running-plate for final fixing. The two outer front lamp brackets are of the extended pattern adopted by the LBSC, whose entire series is included in Edward Beal's *MODELLING THE OLD-TIME RAILWAYS*. The discs are brass, soldered in place and actually show the Victoria to Brighton service. At the bunker, room was found for a strip of lead beneath a cardboard support for the coal. This is fixed by Cromar PVA adhesive, which is invisible when dry.

It is now almost the close of October 2002, when the writer reaches seventy-seven years of his railway life and the matter of Douglas Earle Marsh's finish for the engine has arisen! No luck from the local model shop, but an almost full tin of Gloy R263 Pullman Umber found at home is most promising. The elaborate lining is black with yellow each side and this morning W. H. Smith's produced two biro-type pens of the right colour! The manufacturer is Uni-ball UM – 100 Signo fine, Japanese, and we tested its ability to write on metal on the checkout machine! It will be interesting indeed if the painting is successful of such a rare engine.

The 24th of November was another quite memorable day following Mary's 78th birthday on the 23rd. Vincent Tweed, next door neighbour and leader of our Transport Circle in Ross, had arranged a car-borne visit to both Pendon and Didcot in one day; I think some 160 miles overall. Fortunately, the weather for November was kind, though the River Thames was exceedingly full as we passed by. The writer had never visited Pendon, but had had correspondence with Roye England, the late Founder. We had never met in person although our ideas had much in common. However, the atmosphere in his latest building reflected his own views completely, in that the railway was secondary to the excellent village scene replicas so painstakingly detailed down to the washing on the line and the clearly distinguished rows of vegetables in the cottage gardens.

To the author's surprise we were greeted by the couple who had visited RiMM quite recently, announcing themselves as "drivers at Pendon"! It was a pleasure to stand alongside the complex control panel and watch the lady set some trains in motion. These included their famous coal train of, perhaps, fifty wagons behind Great Western 2-8-0 tender engine. Afterwards the writer asked her who had the job of oiling up all those axleboxes. "I don't think anyone does it," she replied, adding that "some wear out from time to time!" By request, quite a long passenger train behind an LSWR T9 (shudder…) engine ran; the author's conversation being interrupted by a visitor announcing that two coaches had come adrift. Quite consoling to me that even this august operation had its snags. Lady driver took the writer under the basement to seek a stuck relay and into a barn-like underworld some 60ft by 20ft. Another fifteen years' work, her husband estimated, would be necessary to finish this although some running was possible against a rather scant background.

There is no doubt that the Pentroller is a fine piece – ideal for the all-Portescap powered locomotives. Indeed, with both static (like RiMM) and operating trains, enormous amounts of time and money had been invested. The new building has fully controllable mains lighting effects from 'spots' to 'strips' and, as everything is behind glass, was able to create the night time darkness through which ran their lighted train. This showed how little light was available in the English countryside in the 1920s to 30s; this reminds the writer to have another attempt at reconnecting our sets with lighting. It was interesting to note that the coal train employed 3-link couplings (as the real thing) and, indeed, this was stopped and set back so that visitors could see the load being gradually taken up by the locomotive. How the author envied this luxury – only possible where generous curves, estimated around 5ft radius, are practicable.

The couplings on the coaching stock, both static and operational, showed some interesting variations, indicating that RiMM problems of working scale length stock over sharp curves are found even at Pendon. However, the operating stock was close to our 'paper clip and plain hook', but here the connection is disguised to look like steam heating or vacuum pipe. The centre of this is a 'U' section and either end seems to end in a vertical drop-end into each bogie – a method the author adopted many years ago. In effect, the principles are similar and the operation sound – leaving the writer wondering how the two coaches escaped the train we saw – but, it is quite possible some other coupling was also in use.

We exchanged a large bundle of each other's 'flyer' leaflets. The author thinks that the lady driver said their joint run was 120,000; which, with the enormous lighting load downstairs, demonstrates what an expensive business it is to bring really worthwhile work to the notice of the general public. Finally, it seems necessary to record that as everything at Pendon **is** behind glass, there is no opportunity for hands-on-very-close proximity to models that RiMM offers. Indeed, some supervised driving of the trains which we allow is impracticable because the control console is quite beyond the capability of the casual visitor.

As was admitted to the writer, faults do and did occur this day. A considerable team of technical people is needed to maintain such a museum, The death of the founder, Roye England, has left them without a leader currently and the author's concern for the future of RiMM is, perhaps, reflected in the Pendon situation.

On 4th December the author travelled by Stagecoach double-decker bus to Hereford where, with some difficulty, he found his way to the Cider Museum behind Sainsbury's superstore. The purpose was to attend a Forum meeting, which disclosed the expected muddle following the Government apparently trying to combine the functions of museums, archives, libraries and heritage! The members all indicated that they wished to remain 'museums' as a separate entity. Only time will tell what will happen excepting there is continued pressure **not** to satisfactorily **fund**! Mary Sinclair-Powell has replaced Ian Standing and she kindly brought the writer home to Ross. Never had he seen Hereford so choked by cars although we were away **before** the rush hour reached its evening peak! Oh for a simple railway journey in which to relax without the pressures of driving!

Saturday 7th December 2002 found the writer recovering slowly from the celebrations of yesterday's fiftieth wedding anniversary and preparing for another day at RiMM. This was quite an occasion, involving the packing of the LBSC I3 'Atlantic' express tank engine into the transit box. Cleaning the rails had precedence before oiling up two third class Pullman brakes and a first class centre vehicle to make up a train for No. 23. It was indeed a pleasure to couple up and, tentatively, set the engine in motion, replacing a goods train on the down line through Ross. The umber liveried engine and the similarly finished Pullman set made a fine train and hardly completed a circuit before the first visitors arrived.

Being a cold December day, the author thought very few visitors were likely but, after a raisin sandwiches lunch, no less than three batches arrived. Each contingent comprised about four adults and an equal number of children of all ages! Included was a visitor from Spain and locals who had promised their relatives something of a treat to see RiMM. It was rather traumatic to put the new I3 into immediate action but the author decided to risk the rather uncertain 'driving' by the visitors, in contrast with Pendon where all is behind glass. It was twenty to four in the afternoon before the writer could grab a thermos of tea – and prepared to shut down the operation.

Writing this on the Sunday after this 48 hours of most happy, if exhausting activities, the author recalls what a kaleidoscope life has been in the last fifty years... Perhaps most wonderful is the way Mary has put up with my obsession with railways and models throughout our time together; at least, we are **still** together and the grown-up children and grandchildren are so close by. In fact, while the author spent this Saturday in RiMM, Mary was with Natalie and Michelle in the local *Dick Whittington* pantomime... Something for everybody, we might record! And a very happy conclusion to the year.

CHAPTER TEN

The Post-Millenium Year: 2003

T he New Year dawned slowly in dark reality as the trouble with Iraq hovered into the clouds above the world. However, managing RiMM gave little time for depression, since we were open on 2nd January – the first Thursday of 2003. Very few people were about in the streets so some extra cleaning and track level checking took place. Quite surprising as to how much variation in levels takes place due to temperature changes in the room caused by a radiator at each end of the layout – in the area of the tightest radius of the rails! The writer used a 24in steel right-angled ruler, set up on edge across each rail section where difficulty was experienced in current pick-up.

This technique quickly revealed 'dips' and 'hills', which were packed with strips of the one-tenth-of-an-inch cardboard ready to hand. Some of the sections, even pinned down with one-inch pins at about 8in intervals, had pulled loosely upwards; the only practicable realignment being to drill a hole in an adjacent sleeper and reinsert the pin into the Treetex type baseboard.

Successful introduction of the LB&SC I3 locomotive, on a three-car Pullman set, encouraged the writer to consider once more whether yet another engine could be constructed to suit a Hornby 0-6-0 tank engine chassis in the spares box. Again, the criteria were to build something not in preservation full size and also to belong to a pre-1923 Grouping company whose locomotives were not already represented in RiMM. Fate would have it that the writer had kept a drawing of a Glasgow & South Western Railway engine by W. D. Stewart, which appeared in the *Railway Modeller* of February 1977. The Hornby chassis seemed close enough for use as a basis, bearing in mind that tank engines offer some flexibility of wheelbase for replacement of worn out units in the future. The spares box donated the trailing truck and so the 0-6-2 was contrived.

Despite the most extensive trawl through the writer's books and engine files, not a single photograph of this Peter Drummond 1915 locomotive emerged! This was a unique experience for the author – over the years of building, rebuilding etc over forty 4mm scale engines, he had never been without at least one photograph of the chosen one! However, alongside a notice about RiMM in the January 2003 *HMRS News*, is a reference to the Glasgow & South Western Railway Association. Contact with the Chairman, Mr Ian Middledich, has revealed a source of photographs either of No. 45 or her sisters: No.s 84, 90, 91, 122 or 284. He has promised to look out some prints shortly.

Meanwhile, it has been possible to make some items from which this 'general arrangement drawing', together with some photographs of other G & SWR engines provides some guidance. These include the running-plate within which the motor and frame fit, the cab spectacle plates, the brass boiler with smokebox wrapper embossed with rivets, the water fillers (wood) and the front set of double headlamp brackets. The chimney is from chromed brass tubing, a washer base and a brass cupola cut from brass sheet. The dome is made from half-inch wood dowel, carefully fixed with a bolt into the handbrace, shaped with rat tail files. The whistle is from brass one-sixteenth inch tube soldered to steel wire.

The tanks, cab side and bunker appear to be on the same plane and an outline of this has been drawn upon thin card. In effect, this will be a one-piece structure from the front of the tank fitting the boiler and around to the bunker and the offside tank repeated. It is hoped that the photographs will sustain this template; from a photograph of a similar 0-6-4 tank built for the Highland Railway, the joints appear quite sharp, rather than rounded. Basically, sharp joints use less material than generous curves, which could be significant overall. Photographs should help to show how recessed or flush are the cab doors.

The 7th of January 2003 saw a special opening of RiMM for the Glevum Association of Transport Enthusiasts, arranged by Vincent Tweed of our local society. Some of them are working to build a transportable exhibition of 4mm stock upon the 18.86mm gauge and were quite impressed with the museum despite the fact that the gauge is the underscale 16.5mm setting. The author explained that he had tried 18mm gauge in 1943 but, even then, was apprehensive as to the likely problems with outside Walschaert's valve gear and general underframe clearances in stock and track. The Bulldog 'River Fal' demonstrated the incredible 'swing' of the bogies upon the RiMM curves, indicating that a huge area, like Pendon, is necessary to run anything substantial on 18.86 gauge. However, it was an enjoyable evening and the author feels that many matters were interestingly explored. He remains, personally, quite satisfied with the RiMM operation. So many visitors are quite unconcerned as to the precise track gauge, amongst the overall condensation, necessary to show such a layout incorporating a once-existing station etc.

Nothing further emerged from the contact with the G & SWR Association so the writer approached the Historical Model Railway Society and received a photograph of this 0-6-2 tank engine, though in LMS livery – a black and white print with typical Scottish industrial environment setting , but it settled most of the uncertainties. In particular, a one-piece tank side, cab and bunker, repeated on the opposite side, appeared flush with entrance and separate door, recessed and soldered inside.

Repeatedly, visitors seemed quite baffled that no etched brass kits have been used, and listen in disbelief that the author contrives his own kits of parts which are tried out in the thinnest cardboard patterns – before the first pieces of hardware are cut. The increased use of glue, the splendid Evostick 'Impact', has widened the range of materials used in the construction of the engines. Into May 2003, attention has been paid to the only engine the writer considers ever rivalled the Dean single-wheeler of the GWR. It is the Great Eastern P43 Class single of 1898. Although drawings are available in the *Model Railway News* of August 1949, no photographs are to hand. Mr Nock's encyclopedia *British Steam Railways and Locomotives* contains a fine painting, three-quarters off-side; and four excellent prints have been obtained from the HMR Society with help from a local member.

The most difficult item would be to allow sufficient 'swing' on the bogie because the deep outer frame is continuous from front buffer beam to draw-bar at the rear! Cutting out the running-plate, a pivot point was arranged just ahead of the single-wheel; then a mini-frame for the bogie was constructed. Trying this simple combination on the author's wriggling test line immediately showed that the bogie has to be allowed to swing below and **clear** of any outside frame! Indeed, the drawing and photographs showed massive guards over the rear bogie wheels – obviously necessary on the real thing to prevent the flanges cutting through that frame on a tight curve! The solution on the model would be slightly more brutal – the frame would have to be cut through behind the bogie and the front section carried out-rigged on the bogie frame. There would be clearance immediately above this and also at the beginning of the main frame. Of course, this gimmick would be visible on close inspection, but it has solved the problem of negotiating curves down to about 2ft 9ins. The idea of making an 18.83mm gauge version of this engine with a continuous outside frame would, at a guess, require curves of about 6 feet radius!

Having demonstrated an unorthodox practice it occurs to the author that it would be helpful for future modellers to know just what materials are used instead of etched brass, nickel silver and white metal items. Well, GER engine No. 10, a 4-2-2 express type, contains an aluminium boiler (tablet container), lead (sand boxes and weighting), tinplate (talcum powder container and, heavier gauge, metal oilcan), plastic credit card (main splashers, sides and tops, firebox backhead), brass sheet (light cab roof, heavier 1mm spectacle plate and 2mm thick inside frames for driving wheels and trailing pair), brass tubes (below main springs, whistle, tiniest for safety valves), phosphor bronze strip(for pick-ups on driving and trailing wheels, attached to copper-clad plastic strip). Current is supplied to firebox 'oil' flame by old Dublo signal bulb (orange) and through to tender via flexible cable. The latter is one section of flat-typed pair of wires as found linking a radio to an earpiece. The other side of the current to the tender is carried from the engine frame via a flat strip of 5mm phosphor bronze, which engages a vertical bolt and the existing tender coupling. A one-millimetre wide piece of phosphor bronze is soldered upon the flat section and lightly touches both vertical surfaces to ensure continuity of current.

It is now mid-June and Serena has arrived with the very latest camera electronic device which, with three lenses, knocks a tidy hole in £2,000! However, as arranged, she has photographed both engines, GER, No. 10 and G & SWR, No. 102, with all their component parts clearly showing.

Most days at least half an hour is spent with the two engines: painting, rubbing down and repainting. Tiny, about 1mm in diameter, metal thread, gold in finish, was obtained (as a gift!) from a lady's stall at Ross market. It has proved to be ideal for trimming the giant splashers of No. 10. From LFC, 4mm scale name and number plates, 20A Rowe Avenue, Peacehaven, E Sussex, BN10 7PF, most attractive brass cab-side plates were obtained. No. 10 was the only number of the class available, but most delicately finished and secured by Evostick within its oval shape.

Looking at the RiMM catalogue, the writer finds just one GER coach included. This is a brake composite designed for the convenience of passengers travelling to fringes of the line. However, thanks to an unknown contributor at the museum of some old magazines, drawings of the brake third, straight third and a first/third composite – all with corridors – were uncovered. The writer felt that this gift could not be ignored as it would give No. 10 a five-coach set of bogie express stock as representative of the peak of the single-wheelers' lifetime. John Gartside copied these drawings through his special computer and the author supplied the magic 'cartridge' paper, to give two identical copies of each coach side. This amounts to sixteen copies altogether – four for each body – divided into a 'base' sheet and the 'top' lace work in which every panel and frame has to be cut by one-sixteenth inch leather punch (for rounded corners) and scalpel elsewhere.

It is absolutely essential to continuously sharpen the scalpel blade on an oiled stone after every few strokes, applied against a steel triangle or ruler. The side 'base' piece only needs removal of the window apertures. Against a ruler, the base is gently curved 8mm from the bottom edge to give the tumble-home effect to the pair when stuck together. This lamination is carried out with clear wallpaper paste, carefully applied with a small brush to both surfaces. It needs to be allowed to dry out thoroughly and can be laid against a wooden ruler, the contour of which will maintain the tumble-home required. The coach floor is 2mm card and the ends also; over which the printed cartridge paper end is arranged to overlap half a millimetre at the side ends. This will later allow the base/top side sheets to fit in neatly and be Evostuck.

The internal partitions are from lmm card including the corridor sections from which cut-out windows and sliding doors are represented. The seats are folded from thinner material and fitted clear of the outside windows – so allowing room for clear plastic glazing later. The thoroughly dry sides have Ratio brass door handles inserted and stuck. The compartment sides (**not** the corridor sides) are then glued to the base and both ends erected. This technique presents an open shell into which the card compartmental partitions can be added and the fold-out seats inserted. All the interior so far is treated with shellac, which gives strength and a light varnish appearance. The tiny mirrors are from cooking foil aluminium, matching the pictures 8mm by 3.5mm. The third class pictures are sepia brown drawings whereas the first class have coloured pencil sketches and white antimacassars. The much consulted *Home Railways* has a colour plate of a Great Eastern coach, No. 702, to which is added the invaluable information that the first class upholstery is blue cloth with crimson leather in the smoking compartment; the thirds' being crimson and black.

Painting seats and gluing the mirrors and pictures in place is much facilitated at this stage because only the outside compartment side is fitted – so the interior is accessed across the corridor space. The internal doors and window frames can now be added; then the outside corridor side glued to the floor, the partitions and the ends. When all is dry, shellac is applied inside and out. Brass wire .33mm diameter and 9 inches long is obtainable from Alan Gibson and used for the vertical handrails to each door and additionally, horizontally mounted, upon the brake thirds. It was then decided that the shellac only treatment internally was ideal for the compartment divisions, but that the corridor partitions and the inside of the outer sides need a darker shade for which Humbrol Brown No. 186 was applied.

The glazing was added with just a touch of Evostick around each section, cut from a 16mm wide strip of clear plastic. This is best done in approximately 1 inch lengths which terminate half and half at each upright. Longer strips are simply too awkward to fit.

Remember to cut out the plastic where the drop-lights (windows) are modelled 'open'. The seated and the few standing passengers in the corridors need to be added before a test run of roof material is gently fed across the area. These are also cartridge paper, carefully rolled against an 1 inch diameter pole section to start the curve. A steel square drawn along the tops of the partitions' sections will ensure the roof line will be maintained throughout; any bumps being smoothed out with nail file sandpaper strip.

It is useful to make test strips of the cartridge paper, about 1 inch broad, across the roof setting; approximately 40mm wide will be found appropriate to reach from side to side. After the curved nature of the piece has been again fingered against the pole section, just one edge of the roof is treated with Evostick – left a few minutes and then stuck carefully in place. This was then put aside for a day to set. The underframe, of oilcan tinplate, is of L section with the horizontal edge outwards. The headstocks of brass are one millimetre thick. The round section bracing, below, is soldered to vertical rod supports and the solebar. The centre tinplate footboard between the bogies has a steel wire support at each end, also soldered.

The final roofing stage is to Evostick down the other edge and, if available, to lay it into a concave strip of wood former. Secure with light elastic bands and leave for a couple of days. When thoroughly dry a coat of shellac is applied. The tensioning bars are soldered to the solebar and have a split 4mm length of plastic insulation, representing each tensioner, and glued centrally. The vertical drop supports are similarly padded with split insulation (telephone) plastic. The buffers are Evostuck in place as are handmade coupling hooks from hammered copper wire.

The white metal bogies are assembled with Evostick, but the footboards are L shaped tinplate linked also by wire across each end and soldered. The two brake coaches have the author's version of the knuckle coupling at one end, so that any locomotive or 'tail' traffic can be accommodated. Between the carriages are the one-way paper clip couplings; the loop being at the engine end, the following coach having the inverted L of the clip wire, which simply drops into the loop and is very flexible in operation.

These coaches have continuous footboards as GER vehicles upon the solebars' sides. These are scored, with heavy scalpel, upon plastic sheet and snapped against the line while held in smooth jaw pliers. Ends are rounded off and the lengths laid into the solebar on a bed of Evostick. Hold the coach at a sharp angle to check that the boards are level throughout. The aim of the train is to show an important route and the four coaches represent half of the normal Liverpool Street to Cromer set. The route boards were printed by daughter, Serena Robinson, on her computer, font size 6.5, and read "The Norfolk Coast Express Liverpool Street – Cromer". With this font size the overall length of the 'board' is 95mm, which accords with the attachment brackets on the drawings. The upper edge of the boards have a Slater's strip .020in by .030in stuck along against the roof line to give an almost vertical setting.

In conclusion, as Samuel Pepys might have said, "and so to bed" as December 2003 draws to a close. Great Eastern Railway engine No. 10 is standing alongside the four coaches, now in recognisable form, and the anticipation of both the writer and the locomotive is that next year will see them running together in the 'Railways in Miniature' Museum.

CHAPTER ELEVEN

79ᵗʰ Year of Modelling:
2004

E arly in the New Year the writer looked through some magazines kindly donated by visitors. My eye was taken, as they say, by the *Railway Modeller* of December 1986, which contained two of Ian Beattie's drawings entitled 'A Knotty Pair'. They included a handsome 'K' Class 4-4-2 passenger tank engine, of which seven were built between 1911 and 1912, but none have survived in preservation. 'Mainly Trains' of Watchet were contacted for the 24mm 18-spoke Romford wheels, axles, nuts and crankpins plus 9ft 6in coupling rods. They also supplied RiMM's first Japanese motor, a Mashima H 1024 together with a Mainly mounting bracket.

The frames were cut from brass 1.5mm and arranged with horizontal spacers at either end. These were drilled with holes at both ends and aligned with others in the tinplate running-plate. The basic idea was that two bolts only would have nuts so placed as to retain all in place together with the arms of both the bogie and pony truck. The extremely small nature of the driving shaft and worm wheel made security difficult. Eventually the author made a tight fitting washer from glass paper, soaked with Evostick and, being left for a week, really dried solidly.

The cab is unusual in that instead of having a separate roof, it is a one-piece concoction. The best preliminary is to make it in thin white card as a pattern. The front spectacle glasses are quite difficult to make and the writer carried out an experiment by filling them, on a small screwdriver blade, with a soft scraping from the inside of the Cromar PVA adhesive bottle. This dried quite clear and the rear facing glaze also. This has the protective bars laid across before setting the whole upright to set.

The two safety valves are soldered into a 1mm brass base. Between each is the spring from very thin wire, bound around

150

a needle and glued in place. Neither chimney nor dome could be located ready made. The former is brass chromed tube (old child's umbrella) with a solder washer at base and top. The dome is turned from half-inch dowel, with a bolt temporarily through it and locked into the handbrace held in the vice.

The writer decided to have moving connecting rods, of his paddle type, working off soldered eccentric loops on the front driving wheels. This resulted in a motor driving the rear wheels and being set facing the rear. There is little difference in the performance. The bogie follows the usual pattern at RiMM, being two brass side frames soldered to a block of lead – without any pick-up arrangement. This is via a phosphor bronze strip glued to a plastic block between the main frames. This rubs gently upon the wheel tyres.

The livery is crimson lake (Humbrol 20) with Humbrol 69 yellow lining. Completion of this passenger engine and running-in on the layout pointed up the need for a train of suitable non-corridor bogie stock, and by Easter 2004, the work had begun. At first glance this four-coach set c 1912 might appear very ordinary, but it is technically interesting and advanced for the time. It will be noticed that the side door panels on the brake vans are not glazed – hiding the contents from prying eyes. Daylight is provided only by the roof angled glazing panels. These on the model are cut from the corners of a small plastic box.

Common at the time of wooden coachwork is the tumble-home at the waistline, but on these vehicles it is also carried out at each end. Although no gangways were fitted to North Stafford coaches, the first and third composite has short internal corridors to no less than **four** toilets; something of a record in 49ft stock! The company was quick off the mark for electric lighting; the all-third carriage has discs on the roof showing where gas lights were originally fitted. Uniquely, only the NSR brake vans were fitted with the dynamos and double-batteries; connecting high-level leads joined coach to coach and so were not interchangeable with other companies' stock.

Construction followed the laminated principles previously outlined. Three drawings: a composite, straight-third, and a four-compartment brake, are found in the *Historic Carriage Drawings*

Volume 1, LMS and LNER by Jenkinson and Camping. The second brake third, with only two passenger compartments, appeared in the July 1962 edition of the *Model Railway Constructor*, drawn by Ian R Smith. All items necessary to buy in were obtained from Mainly Trains of Watchett, West Somerset. The torpedo vents are ABS LMS 700, the door handles are Roxey 4A 108 and the L-shaped grab rails are 4A 118 SECR.

The unusual 8ft wheelbase bogies are Ratio LNWR, with Jackson 14mm pinpoint disc wheels. On assembly, the oil cap covers are rehung to the left as was the NSR practice. The coach interiors are fitted out with partitions in the composite, upholstery in the first being blue cloth, with brown or red in the thirds. The two sets of brake duckets are filed and cut from clear plastic. The outside body finish was described as 'madder lake' with centrally mounted NSR crest. Lining is black edged with a thin yellow line. The writer has given some thought to the provision or otherwise of the fine yellow lines on panelling; if this on the prototype was only three-eighths of an inch, modelling on the one-seventysixth scale would be virtually invisible! Repetition of THIRD (32 times!) and FIRST in full on every door seems unavoidable for the pre-1923 era. After that time simple '3' or '1' on the doors was clearly a cheap alternative and much easier for the modeller.

It is worthwhile finishing the roofs of a set differently for logical reasons e.g. the third newly fitted with electric lighting with the gas entries blocked is painted matt white Humbrol 36. The colour won't last long but, never mind; the composite which would receive more attention than other vehicles is matt off-white Humbrol 28. The brakes both have medium grey finish and is Gloy ST/M/44 dark grey. Some suitable painted numbers for all the vehicles will be found with the drawings for either North Staffords or LMS eras.

In July 2004, *Railway Modellers* of November 1962 and August 1976 came to the writer's notice, displaying drawings of a Great Eastern Railway 3-plank wagon. A simple vehicle, but built for military traffic during World War I 1914–18, it was cleverly designed with not only drop sides but also drop ends. Such a handy wagon was well worth modelling and an Estate Book of 1910 gave details of a two-wheeled water tank which was made as the load. Information with the drawings noted that the Great

Eastern ropes carried a red strand for identification of the owning company to deter theft. This feature caused much interest when the little wagon appeared on the World War I train.

By August 2004 the writer was drawn to the creation of a massive engine for freight haulage at the museum. The inspiration was *Modern Locomotive Classes* by Brian Reed, Locomotive Publishing Co Ltd, Westminster, London and purchased in August 1945. It contains an early photograph of the LMS 1927 2-6-0 & 0-6-2 Beyer-Garratt plus an excellent drawing of the later rotating coal bunker (powered by a small 2 cylinder steam engine), modification which all thirty-three engines received by 1930. They were designed to include standard details of LMS 2-6-0 engines, fortunately and the Hornby 2 cylinder Fowler R 2397 2-6-4 tank engines have appropriate wheelbase and were obtained from East Kent Models of Whitstable as powered chassis.

An essential book for this work is *LMS & LNER Garratts* by Essery and Toms, published by Wild Swan. this contains photographs of every engine built. Fortunately, Brian Reed's slim book includes a drawing of the Garratt in fully developed stage i.e. with the revolving coal bunker, and this was enlarged to give a 4mm scale print of the monster! Receipt of the powered mechanisms enabled examination of how the water tank end and coal bunker would 'fit' the Hornby work. Admiring the beautiful Walschearts gear, the writer saw just how right are most RTR manufacturers in sticking to 16.5mm gauge!

Basically, the upperworks are erected upon **brass** sheet running-plate; an experiment in tinplate was abandoned as it was immediately slapped against the motor housing. The conic frustrum shaped coal bunker and the main water tank are mainly brass. Don't tell the Treasury, but the ends of the bunker contain 1p and 5p coins soldered in place! Both units have room for lead strip to increase adhesion. Certain small fittings, tank fillers, lifting lugs, strapping, doors etc, are made from vinyl, thin card and tinplate, Evostuck in position.

The centrepiece is the big boiler on its quite massive frame. There is an important action at this stage; just putting each chassis back-to-back on the track will reveal an immediate **short** if they touch! This is because the 'common' side of the chassis is reversed because one half is facing forward, the other backward. The solution, however, is simple: the centrepiece must have insulated couplings; in the author's case, flat brass strip to bolts which are set into the plastic curtain rail used to represent the frame.

The big boiler is a happy right diameter length of copper piping soldered into a tinplate Belpaire firebox. There is no fear of magnetic influence in this area and the cab and running-plate are tinplate, with a thin brass sheet roof fixed on with Evostick. This roof section is first bound by elastic bands to a small pot, for a couple of days, to ensure that it 'sits' comfortably when Evostuck. If you wish to model the roof vents 'open' this must be cut on the bench before fitting. The vertical handrails, either side of the door, have a bent upper section so that it fits closely when Evostuck under the cab roof. Also glue to the running-plate at the foot.

In vain the writer sought a suitable chimney, dome and 4-stem Ross safety valves unit. One regrets the very limited range of such castings from the trade early on, but they were usually illustrated in the catalogue. Today, unless one has the electronic machine, all we have is a written note which still leaves the builder guessing whether or not it meets the need. So, back to the primitive. Tube (ex-child's umbrella) was found the right diameter for the chimney with a thin washer gently bent over copper tube to 'seat'. The cupola (rim) is a filed out washer (gently, with rat tail) to be a push fit secured with Evostick.

The dome was turned in the drill brace from about 14mm length of half-inch diameter wooden dowel, held in the brace by a bolt through the centre and locked with a nut. Steady work with a flat file reduces the centre to the correct diameter (check with a micrometer if you've got one) while the splayed out seating is also shaped with rat tail files. Not surprisingly, with such a massive boiler, the safety valve has four stems cut from 1mm steel tube – a gift from a neighbour. The base is 1mm, brass with the four valves tapped into lmm holes as a push fit. This area is then flooded with solder and quickly breathed on to 'set' the whole.

All three components are Evostuck in position. This prevents the substantial problem of soldering to such a heavy copper tube and (for the chimney) fixing to the very thin card wrapper surround; the rivets on which are pressed by a blunt needle held in a pin chuck. This technique is used on both the water tank (end access plates), the grate area, on the frame above the pony trucks and also on the wrappers around the rotating coal bunker. All such additions are treated with shellac to preserve the raised rivets and the non-metal material overall.

At this stage the simple flat brass couplings, through which the vertical bolts of the chassis and running-plates run, were coupled up for a trial run of the three components. This exciting moment confirmed that the boiler section isolated the two powered units from each other and so there was no 'shorting' – just the smooth movement to left or right on the small test track. An orange 12 volt bulb in the firebox, connecting across the coupling bolts, added to the effect in the twilight! Between the bunker and the engine is the large, circular coal feed. This is made from black fabric rolled around a piece of dowel and stuck to form a tube which links the two units by pushing into each. Leave loose so that it may be removed to give access to the bolt below.

Attention can now move, in the sixth month of building, to the vulnerable fittings (centre section foot steps, the 'V' below frame etc) and the filling in of the spectacle plate windows with PVA, which dries quite clearly as glass. The finish will be 1937ish LMS black. Careful examination of the LMS & LNER Garratt book pages, showing at least one view of each engine built, does show typical freight finish – largely dirt! It is likely that the horizontal surfaces, and also the area around the coal bunker will be toned with dark grey, both for contrast and realism. The lettering, number 4975, company initials, are shown in a coloured sheet which appeared in the *Model Railway Constructor* of August 1975.

The decision as to which running number to apply was influenced by the need to increase the size of the water tank to contain the Hornby mechanism. It is recorded that larger tanks were fitted to at least some engines, but the only positive evidence appears in the photographs, among which No. 4975 seemed appropriate. It is now the end of January 2005, and the builder has decided to leave this Bayer Garratt in its multicolour/multimaterial nude state in order that viewers may have some idea of the construction. A final touch is the smoke! This is faked by teasing out a cotton bud and glueing the end to a piece of lead shot. this drops down the chimney while the cotton haze blows in the breeze created by running the engine. Experimentally fitted to another engine in the museum, this was looked on with some surprise by visitors!

CHAPTER TWELVE

The Author's 80ᵗʰ Birthday: 2005

A t the turn of the New Year, the author was conscious of how poorly we are served by distant memories of the pre-Grouping companies, when he came across a page of the *Railway Modeller*, dated February 1977. A small 'Bleak Winter Day' photograph showed Furness Railway No. 118, a huge 4-6-4 tank, leaving Kitson's Works in 1920. Hunting through RiMM's considerable records revealed no further information so approaches to other sources began. Through the Historical Model Railway Society the Furness Railway steward, Michael Peascod, was contacted and much information, including a Works Drawing, arrived. From the National Railway Museum Library at York appeared a drawing from the *Railway Modeller* of January 1977, another from page 116 of 1966, and a print from the April 1939 *Model Railway Constructor*; from *The Locomotive* of April 1921, a further drawing of No. 85 and a photograph of No. 115.

No less than five 4mm drawings of this enormous 'Baltic' tank – a luxury the writer cannot recall happening in over sixty years modelling! Four photographs from the National Railway Museum are frequently viewed because (have **you** had this experience?) the bundle of drawings **do** vary in detail – which is surprising as only five such locomotives were built. After the 'Thank you' letters, attention turned to the matter of a British commercial mechanism, if available, to ensure replacement in the future, rather than building a 'one-off' with Japanese motor. Choice fell upon the Hornby LNER B12 R 2320 motorised chassis and this was supplied by East Kent Models at £27.50 plus £2 postage.

The motor, as mounted, has just sufficient boiler clearance and two locations: fore and (vertical) aft, which will permit simple bolt attachment to the running-plate. The running-plate has a substantial cut-out area around the motor and the soldered vallance, of strip phosphor bronze, is quite tricky to fit as the running-plate drops down immediately below the firebox. The spectacle plates are one millimetre brass and the front one is more 'air' than material in order to accommodate the Belpaire firebox and the four spectacle frame windows. The above-the-running-plate sections of the frames are weirdly shaped and well worth making first in thin white card as a pattern.

Perhaps the most massive structure the writer has ever made is one piece of Castrol Oil tinplate can, almost 12in long (!) which forms the wrap-around tanks and bunker section. The most difficult part is cutting and filing the bottom section immediately below the cab where the vallance drops. Again, a thin card pattern will serve well to avoid error. The entrance is entirely cut out, apart from the lower 4mm step and the door, with folded top edge, is soldered in place from the inside. Note that two horizontal handrail holes are required at the cab side front, and a rear handrail and lamp brackets are required at the bunker rear. When this is all soldered in place, hammered .029 wire is flattened as trim and soldered around the top edges and cab entrance.

The firebox, only about one-third its actual depth, must be of brass due to the nearness of the motor; big pins and small ones being soldered through holes to represent stays and washout plugs. Hunting for correct diameter copper tube for the boiler revealed a heavy plastic section – the origin of which is unknown. This was cut to fit in length between smokebox door and a 4mm addition to Evostick beneath the firebox front edge. The door is a rubbed down button with the thread holes filled with filler.

Upon the running-plate, and soldered in place, are sections of frame between which sits a wooden smokebox saddle. This is Evostuck and prevents any solder work disturbance. Rivets are rather prominent in this engine and are made upon fine quality paper impressed by a blunt needle held in a pin-vice. The longest section is that upon the lower tank and bunker side. After punching, a fine strip of paper, just over a millimetre wide, is cut out with a very sharp scalpel drawn along a steel straight edge. This is secured with PVA applied with a small paintbrush and although this may be cheating, it is easier than punching the metal unless you have specialised equipment. Other areas similarly treated are the frame section above the running-plate, alongside the smokebox and between the wheels of both bogies.

Leave at least 24 hours, then stir up the shellac and gently paint along the strips to set and strengthen the rivets permanently.

The 'signature' of an engine is the chimney and photographs help to bring the drawings to life – also of the dome and the twin valve safety valve. Ex-brass tube from children's umbrellas or time-expired radio aerials are an excellent source of chimneys. The chrome finish should be rubbed off to give a 'key' to the two washers, one at each end of the chimney. The lower one must be bent carefully to seat upon the smokebox wrapper, the latter being of fine card in this instance. Both washers are soldered in place with sufficient solder to build up the curves. Cut a 4mm wide strip of glass cloth and, **before** cutting the chimney from its host tube, pull the strip of abrasive back and forward to match the taper in the drawings and photographs.

The dome is again a section of half-inch dowel through which a bolt is fitted and held in the chuck of the hand drill erected horizontally in the vice. The shaping of the dome is carried out with a range of files and glass paper until the sides, top and saddle to fit the boiler is achieved. The trade does not show photographs of their components in their lists and unless your locomotive is a well-known Big Four design, it isn't possible to judge whether a ready made version is available. The brass cased safety valves is a carefully squeezed hollow rivet in the vice. The twin valves are of the finest tube available (possibly medical source), set in a 'bath' of Evostick.

Additional weight to that associated with the Hornby motor was added; the smokebox and boiler in front of the mechanism being filled with some obsolete brass pins from old 15 amp plugs; balsa and Evostick securing. Both sides of the water tank contain lead flashing strips Evostuck in place. These also prevent the tinplate tank sides from interfering with the motor's magnetic field. At this stage the model is supported by a length of dowel about its centrepoint. This is used to judge the weight of lead/brass bits to put into the coal bunker to ensure the engine is neatly balanced for steady running.

As earlier mentioned, some five drawings of this locomotive came to hand and it is often necessary to compare measurements to decide which one you will use! The water filling cap is an uncertainty as to top fittings. The writer sorted this out by copying a photograph since the draughtmen's design seemed rather notional. The size/shape of the rear portals and the layout of the bunker end produced further variations and no drawing showed the cab rain strip. This is almost inevitable, indicating that some detail was missing when the drawings were made so long after the prototype had vanished. Contractors were also likely to make a few variations where uncertainties existed.

Disappointed in the shallow depth of a brass nameplate recently obtained, the author decided to make both the bunker numberplate and the maker's plate, which is situated upon the above running-plate frame, below the smokebox. This was cut out in brass and filed as near as possible to follow both photographic and drawing evidence. After fixing in place, with Evostick, the black background paint is applied leaving the letters, numbers and edging (in this case 118, the engine with the longest life – until 1940) in the brass. These will need touching up with brass paint applied with the smallest brush and viewed through a magnifying glass.

No Humbrol primer was available locally but the writer found Hammerite special metals primer, although not for ferrous metals, gave a sound red/brown finish overall. The only Furness locomotive paint located is by Precision, in matt (dull) P 800 Furness locomotive red. This was obtained from Mainly Trains, who also supplied the Furness blue and white for the coaches. It is worth setting the body on the Hornby chassis at this stage to make sure no additions have fouled the smooth running. Slow speed immediately indicated a fault. Upturning all and applying current to the wheels showed two 'snags' as the RAF say. One was that a spring brass wire impacting on a rear driver, collecting firebox bulb current, was pressed against it by the balsa wood block behind the firebox backhead. This had settled a little lower than intended and also rubbed the rear driving wheel flanges. Some attention with a scalpel showed the wisdom of not using oak or other hardwood in such places. The running is now very encouraging and the brass and lead weights provide an overall weight of 20oz on the driving wheels. Quite the biggest and heaviest locomotive ever made by the writer – Castrol oil and grease must be lightly applied! If cellophane can be found with black lines printed upon it, this is a convenient base on which to add the red lines each side and so form the boiler bands fixed on with a little gloss varnish underneath. A source of the Furness coat-of-arms is the *British Steam Railways & Locomotives* by O. S. Nock: a coloured plate No. 179.

The collection of drawings and photographs for a train for No. 118 was scarce indeed, amounting to a drawing in Edward Beal's *MODELLING THE OLD-TIME RAILWAYS*, which the writer reproduced to 4mm scale and amended two compartments of the 6-wheeled thirds so that they became the front and rear brakes. The 6-wheeled third, referred to above, is included on page 45 of *Historic Carriage Drawings LMS and LNER*, which also has a half-section side elevation of a 49ft non-corridor bogie third. Juggling of eight reproductions upon cartridge paper enabled sides to be made and assembled upon the card base floors. Cromar PVA white adhesive was used to effect this with 3mm strips of cartridge paper to lap the several joints internally.

A non-corridor 47ft bogie first/third composite drawing was found in *Model Railways* of April 1980, but this is overscale and must be reduced before reproducing on cartridge paper. Construction proceeded as outlined earlier on other coaches, with metal underframe from no longer available metal car oil tins. Both 8ft bogies and the tapered, round head buffers, are by Bachmann via Mainly Trains. The bogies come complete with wheels for 16.5 gauge, but require a 3mm diameter pivot with rubbing cylinder of 5mm, which is glued to the flat strip joining both solebars. All wheels are painted brownish red to indicate Mansell wood centres.

The composite has short corridors and separate lavatories for first and third. Remember to paint the windows white and fit handrails along the inside of the corridor sections before the roof is fitted. All compartment divisions are in place and it is a nice check to lay a steel square from one end to the other tops. Use a card nail file to reduce any high points. This procedure will ensure that the roof, cartridge paper in this case, fits closely. Apply Evostick to the upper ridge of one side only, also along the roof edge. Carefully attach and leave to dry for 24 hours. This technique enables the roof to be 'tried' as to fit before adding glue to compartment tops and trimming the remaining side.

161

The available drawings ignore the lighting , but a photograph on page 71 in *Railway Carriage Album* shows two gas cylinders, mounted line-astern, approximately 5ft long each; as fitted to a 49' Furness composite of 1906. Both bogies' coaches have two dowel tanks with one each on the brake van six-wheelers. The latter bodies are mounted on two Hornby 6-wheel sausage van chassis, with the rather brutal 'Clement' system replaced by two, hand-wound, light springs which suspend the central wheels in gentle contact with curves. The centre brake blocks are cut off as inapplicable. A good photograph of a six-wheeled brake No. 13 is shown on page 114 of *British Railway Carriages of the 20th Century, Volume 1.*

The ends of the coaches are panelled, and this is worth doing as there are no corridor connections to divert attention. The vacuum pipes between the coaches have a reverse bend and reach towards each other without actual connection; from the side viewing this break is not obvious. My paper-clip loop and drop-in couplings are fitted to all. The coaches have seating (reddish in thirds, blue in the firsts) with photographs, sepia in the thirds and coloured in the firsts, also passengers, most of whom are reading papers.

The footboards, being vulnerable in handling, are Evostuck as the painting (including eighteen coats-of-arms!) is concluded. Plastic, from date boxes, is the footboard material, glued against the solebars. The central, lower, footboards on both bogie coaches are cut and folded tinplate soldered to 14mm pins pushed and glued into the floors. The gas tanks have 14mm pins, with filed flat heads as the gauges. These are black painted then over-painted white with the pointer scratched through with a pin-vice.

Referring again to Edward Beal's *Modelling the Old Time Railways* revealed a drawing by R D Pochin, of an early horse box which might make a neat item of tail-traffic for this short train. Fortunately, the stock of 'bits and pieces' revealed a set of MJT 4ft 6in axleguards and springs, also the small 3ft (12mm) disc wheels of the prototype. These would fit a MJT frame within a tinplate tray type of underfloor and with solebars bent down. these are plainly wood in the prototype. This also included an early single-sided wood block handbrake, which was obviously inadequate for running in the comparatively modern passenger train.

Happily, the Edward Beal book also contains two drawings of London & South Western horse boxes, one of which is a short version much like the Furness in question. From this it was possible to derive a set of brake gears with vacuum cylinder and handbrake on both sides. The box-like body, with no tumble-home, is made from one millimetre cardboard. The Pochin drawing was enlarged to 4mm scale on cartridge paper, which was stuck with PVA adhesive to the cardboard. Don't forget to cut an over-generous opening on the 'box' to contain clear plastic for the single window. Painting this frame brown first will prevent spillage on the plastic. The cast oil lamp and ventilators are added to the very thin card roof.

It will become obvious that although the copied side of the drawing provides one complete side of the van, it is necessary to make vertical cuts in three places and reverse the position of doors to match the opposite side. PVA will make a neat job and hide the joints. The whole is shellacked and, when thoroughly dry, the coach blue is applied. The printed lettering F R and 17, are touched up with yellow paint. The four coaches and the horse box make a little train to which engine No. 118 provides a massive contrast in Furness red, against the blue and white rolling stock.

Small showcases are ready at 'Chase Side' for both the Great Western Railway 'River Fal' engine, with typical three-coach stock for the Gloucester–Ross–Hereford train, and this Furness set, which is likely to be my final effort to portray the steam age in Britain.

APPENDUM

This is the story of one man's representation of the middle years of British railways, culminating in the 'Railways in Miniature' Museum, the last shown free to the public at Ross-on-Wye, and which has now reached a critical state as to its future.

Unfortunately, the author's single-handed curating, maintaining and producing of new trains has also ceased due to his ill health. Consequently, RiMM has had to be closed.

This has been compounded by the offering for sale of the building housing the museum, but, thanks to wide ranging local news coverage, the future of 'Railways in Miniature' is now likely to be secured by new ownership in a neighbouring location.

RiMM is in a course of establishment at Dick Whittington Farm Park, Little London, Longhope, Gloucestershire with planned re-opening it to the public by Christmas 2008.

INDEX

This work includes all the engines and rolling stock made and described in the *Railways in Miniature* museum catalogue, not all of which are mentioned in this book.

P

R